RESUMES
FOR
MID-CAREER
JOB CHANGES

RESUMES
FOR
MID-CAREER
JOB CHANGES

The Editors of
VGM Career Horizons

Second Edition

VGM Career Horizons
NTC/Contemporary Publishing Group

Library of Congress Cataloging-in-Publication Data

Resumes for mid-career job changes / the editors of VGM Career
    Horizons ; revised by Kathy Siebel.—2nd ed.
        p.   cm. — (VGM professional resumes series)
    Rev. ed. of: Resumes for mid-career job changes. c1993.
    ISBN 0-8442-2950-4
    1. Résumés (Employment)   I. VGM Career Horizons (Firm)
II. Title: Resumes for mid-career job changes.   III. Series.
HF5383.R445   1999
    808'.066651—dc21   99-21574
                                                          CIP

We would like to acknowledge the assistance of Kathy Siebel
in compiling and editing this book.

Interior design by City Desktop Productions, Inc.

Published by VGM Career Horizons
A division of NTC/Contemporary Publishing Group, Inc.
4255 West Touhy Avenue, Lincolnwood (Chicago), Illinois 60712-1975 U.S.A.
Printed in the United States of America
International Standard Book Number: 0-8442-2950-4

00 01 02 03 04 05 VL 19 18 17 16 15 14 13 12 11 10 9 8 7 6 5 4 3 2 1

Contents

Introduction

Your resume is your first impression on a prospective employer. Though you may be articulate, intelligent, and charming in person, a poor resume may prevent you from ever having the opportunity to demonstrate your interpersonal skills, because a poor resume may prevent you from ever being called for an interview. While few people have ever been hired solely on the basis of their resume, a well-written, well-organized resume can go a long way toward helping you land an interview. Your resume's main purpose is to get you that interview. The rest is up to you and the employer. If you both feel that you are right for the job and the job is right for you, chances are you will be hired.

A resume must catch the reader's attention yet still be easy to read and to the point. Resume styles have changed over the years. Today, brief and focused resumes are preferred. No longer do employers have the patience, or the time, to review several pages of solid type. A resume should be only one page long, if possible. Time is a precious commodity in today's business world and the resume that is concise and straightforward will usually be the one that gets noticed.

Let's not make the mistake, though, of assuming that writing a brief resume means that you can take less care in preparing it. A successful resume takes time and thought, and if you are willing to make the effort, the rewards are well worth it. Think of your resume as a sales tool with the product being you. You want to sell yourself to a prospective employer. This book is designed to help you prepare a resume that will help you further your career—to land that next job, or first job, or to return to the workforce after years of absence. So, read on. Make the effort and reap the rewards that a strong resume can bring to your career. Let's get to it!

The Elements of a Good Resume

A winning resume is made of the elements that employers are most interested in seeing when reviewing a job applicant. These basic elements are the essential ingredients of a successful resume and become the actual sections of your resume. The following is a list of elements that may be used in a resume. Some are essential, some are optional. We will be discussing these in this chapter in order to give you a better understanding of each element's role in the makeup of your resume:

1. Heading

2. Objective

3. Work Experience

4. Education

5. Honors

6. Activities

7. Certificates and Licenses

8. Professional Memberships

9. Special Skills

10. Personal Information

11. References

The first step in preparing your resume is to gather information about yourself and your past accomplishments. Later you will refine this information, rewrite it in the most effective language, and organize it into the most attractive layout. First, let's take a look at each of these important elements individually.

Heading

The heading may seem to be a simple enough element in your resume, but be careful not to take it lightly. The heading should be placed at the top of your resume and should include your name, home address, and telephone numbers. If you can take calls at your current place of business, include your business number, since most employers will attempt to contact you during the business day. If this is not possible, or if you can afford it, purchase an answering machine that allows you to retrieve your messages while you are away from home. This way you can make sure you don't miss important phone calls. Always include your phone number on your resume. It is crucial that when prospective employers need to have immediate contact with you, they can.

Objective

When seeking a particular career path, it is important to list a job objective on your resume. This statement helps employers know the direction that you see yourself heading, so that they can determine whether your goals are in line with the position available. The objective is normally one sentence long and describes your employment goals clearly and concisely. See the sample resumes in this book for examples of objective statements.

The job objective will vary depending on the type of person you are, the field you are in, and the type of goals you have. It can be either specific or general, but it should always be to the point.

In some cases, this element is not necessary, but usually it is a good idea to include your objective. It gives your possible future employer an idea of where you are coming from and where you want to go.

The objective statement is better left out, however, if you are uncertain of the exact title of the job you seek. In such a case, the inclusion of an overly specific objective statement could result in your not being considered for a variety of acceptable positions; be sure to incorporate this information in your cover letter instead.

Work Experience

This element is arguably the most important of them all. It will provide the central focus of your resume, so it is necessary that this section be as complete as possible. Only by examining your work experience in depth can you get to the heart of your accomplishments and present them in a way that demonstrates the strength of your qualifications. Of course, someone just out of school will have less work experience than someone who has been working for a number of years, but the amount of information isn't the most important thing—rather, how it is presented, and how it highlights you as a person and as a worker will be what counts.

As you work on this section of your resume, be aware of the need for accuracy. You'll want to include all necessary information about each of your jobs, including job title, dates, employer, city, state, responsibilities, special projects, and accomplishments. Be sure to only list company accomplishments for which you were directly responsible. If you haven't participated in any special projects, that's all right—this area may not be relevant to certain jobs.

The most common way to list your work experience is in *reverse chronological order*. In other words, start with your most recent job and work your way backward. This way your prospective employer sees your current (and often most important) job before seeing your past jobs. Your most recent position, if the most important, should also be the one that includes the most information, as compared to your previous positions. If you are just out of school, show your summer employment and part-time work, though in this case your education will most likely be more important than your work experience.

The following worksheets will help you gather information about your past jobs.

WORK EXPERIENCE

Job One:

Job Title _____

Dates _____

Employer _____

City, State _____

Major Duties _____

_____

_____

_____

_____

_____

_____

_____

_____

Special Projects _____

_____

_____

_____

Accomplishments _____

_____

_____

_____

_____

_____

_____

_____

Job Two:

Job Title _____

Dates _____

Employer _____

City, State _____

Major Duties _____

_____

_____

_____

_____

_____

_____

_____

Special Projects _____

_____

_____

_____

Accomplishments _____

_____

_____

_____

_____

_____

_____

_____

_____

Job Three:

Job Title _____

Dates _____

Employer _____

City, State _____

Major Duties _____

_____

_____

_____

_____

_____

_____

_____

Special Projects _____

_____

_____

_____

Accomplishments _____

_____

_____

_____

_____

_____

_____

_____

Job Four:

Job Title _____

Dates _____

Employer _____

City, State _____

Major Duties _____

_____

_____

_____

_____

_____

_____

Special Projects _____

_____

_____

_____

Accomplishments _____

_____

_____

_____

_____

_____

_____

_____

Education

Education is the second most important element of a resume. Your educational background is often a deciding factor in an employer's decision to hire you. Be sure to stress your accomplishments in school with the same finesse that you stressed your accomplishments at work. If you are looking for your first job, your education will be your greatest asset, since your work experience will most likely be minimal. In this case, the education section becomes the most important. You will want to be sure to include any degrees or certificates you received, your major area of concentration, any honors, and any relevant activities. Again, be sure to list your most recent schooling first. If you have completed graduate-level work, begin with that and work in reverse chronological order through your undergraduate education. If you have completed an undergraduate degree, you may choose whether to list your high school experience or not. This should be done only if your high school grade point average was well above average.

The following worksheets will help you gather information for this section of your resume. Also included are supplemental worksheets for honors and for activities. Sometimes honors and activities are listed in a section separate from education, most often near the end of the resume.

EDUCATION

School One _____

Major or Area of Concentration _____

Degree _____

Dates _____

School Two _____

Major or Area of Concentration _____

Degree _____

Dates _____

Honors

Here you should list any awards, honors, or memberships in honorary societies that you have received. Usually these are of an academic nature, but they can also be for special achievement in sports, clubs, or other school activities. Always be sure to include the name of the organization honoring you and the date(s) received. Use the worksheet below to help gather your honors information.

HONORS

Honor One _____

Awarding Organization _____

Date(s) _____

Honor Two _____

Awarding Organization _____

Date(s) _____

Honor Three _____

Awarding Organization _____

Date(s) _____

Honor Four _____

Awarding Organization _____

Date(s) _____

Activities

You may have been active in different organizations or clubs during your years at school; often an employer will look at such involvement as evidence of initiative and dedication. Your ability to take an active role, and even a leadership role, in a group should be included on your resume. Use the worksheet provided to list your activities and accomplishments in this area. In general, you should exclude any organization whose name indicates the race, creed, sex, age, marital status, color, or nation of origin of its members.

ACTIVITIES

Organization/Activity _____

Accomplishments _____

_____

_____

Organization/Activity _____

Accomplishments _____

_____

_____

Organization/Activity _____

Accomplishments _____

_____

_____

Organization/Activity _____

Accomplishments _____

_____

_____

As your work experience increases through the years, your school activities and honors will play less of a role in your resume, and eventually you will most likely only list your degree and any major honors you received. This is due to the fact that, as time goes by, your job performance becomes the most important element in your resume. Through time, your resume should change to reflect this.

Certificates and Licenses

The next potential element of your resume is certificates and licenses. You should list these if the job you are seeking requires them and you, of course, have acquired them. If you have applied for a license, but have not yet received it, use the phrase "application pending."

License requirements vary by state. If you have moved or you are planning to move to another state, be sure to check with that state's board or licensing agency to be sure that you are aware of all licensing requirements.

Always be sure that all of the information you list is completely accurate. Locate copies of your licenses and certificates and check the exact date and name of the accrediting agency. Use the following worksheet to list your licenses and certificates.

CERTIFICATES AND LICENSES

Name of License _____

Licensing Agency _____

Date Issued _____

Name of License _____

Licensing Agency _____

Date Issued _____

Name of License _____

Licensing Agency _____

Date Issued _____

Professional Memberships

Another potential element in your resume is a section listing professional memberships. Use this section to list involvement in professional associations, unions, and similar organizations. It is to your advantage to list any professional memberships that pertain to the job you are seeking. Be sure to include the dates of your involvement and whether you took part in any special activities or held any offices within the organization. Use the following worksheet to gather your information.

PROFESSIONAL MEMBERSHIPS

Name of Organization _____

Offices Held _____

Activities _____

Dates _____

Name of Organization _____

Offices Held _____

Activities _____

Dates _____

Name of Organization _____

Offices Held _____

Activities _____

Dates _____

Name of Organization _____

Offices Held _____

Activities _____

Dates _____

Special Skills

This section of your resume is set aside for mentioning any special abilities you have that could relate to the job you are seeking. This is the part of your resume where you have the opportunity to demonstrate certain talents and experiences that are not necessarily a part of your educational or work experience. Common examples include fluency in a foreign language, or knowledge of a particular computer application.

Special skills can encompass a wide range of your talents—remember to be sure that whatever skills you list relate to the type of work you are looking for.

Personal Information

Some people include "Personal" information on their resumes. This is not generally recommended, but you might wish to include it if you think that something in your personal life, such as a hobby or talent, has some bearing on the position you are seeking. This type of information is often referred to at the beginning of an interview, when it is used as an "ice breaker." Of course, personal information regarding age, marital status, race, religion, or sexual preference should never appear on any resume.

References

References are not usually listed on the resume, but a prospective employer needs to know that you have references who may be contacted if necessary. All that is necessary to include in your resume regarding references is a sentence at the bottom stating, "References are available upon request." If a prospective employer requests a list of references, be sure to have one ready. Also, check with whomever you list to see if it is all right for you to use them as a reference. Forewarn them that they may receive a call regarding a reference for you. This way they can be prepared to give you the best reference possible.

Chapter 2

Writing Your Resume

Now that you have gathered all of the information for each of the sections of your resume, it's time to write out each section in a way that will get the attention of whoever is reviewing it. The type of language you use in your resume will affect its success. You want to take the information you have gathered and translate it into a language that will cause a potential employer to sit up and take notice.

Resume writing is not like expository writing or creative writing. It embodies a functional, direct writing style and focuses on the use of action words. By using action words in your writing, you more effectively stress past accomplishments. Action words help demonstrate your initiative and highlight your talents. Always use verbs that show strength and reflect the qualities of a "doer." By using action words, you characterize yourself as a person who takes action, and this will impress potential employers.

The following is a list of verbs commonly used in resume writing. Use this list to choose the action words that can help your resume become a strong one:

administered	billed
advised	built
analyzed	carried out
arranged	channeled
assembled	collected
assumed responsibility	communicated

compiled	maintained
completed	managed
conducted	met with
contacted	motivated
contracted	negotiated
coordinated	operated
counseled	orchestrated
created	ordered
cut	organized
designed	oversaw
determined	performed
developed	planned
directed	prepared
dispatched	presented
distributed	produced
documented	programmed
edited	published
established	purchased
expanded	recommended
functioned as	recorded
gathered	reduced
handled	referred
hired	represented
implemented	researched
improved	reviewed
inspected	saved
interviewed	screened
introduced	served as
invented	served on

sold	tested
suggested	trained
supervised	typed
taught	wrote

Now take a look at the information you put down on the work experience worksheets. Take that information and rewrite it in paragraph form, using verbs to highlight your actions and accomplishments. Let's look at an example, remembering that what matters here is the writing style, and not the particular job responsibilities given in our sample.

WORK EXPERIENCE
Regional Sales Manager

Manager of sales representatives from seven states. Responsible for twelve food chain accounts in the East. In charge of directing the sales force in planned selling toward specific goals. Supervisor and trainer of new sales representatives. Consulting for customers in the areas of inventory management and quality control.

Special Projects: Coordinator and sponsor of annual food industry sales seminar.

Accomplishments: Monthly regional volume went up 25 percent during my tenure while, at the same time, a proper sales/cost ratio was maintained. Customer/company relations improved significantly.

Below is the rewritten version of this information, using action words. Notice how much stronger it sounds.

WORK EXPERIENCE
Regional Sales Manager

Managed sales representatives from seven states. Handled twelve food chain accounts in the eastern United States. Directed the sales force in planned selling toward specific goals. Supervised and trained new sales representatives. Consulted for customers in the areas of inventory management and quality control. Coordinated and sponsored the annual Food Industry Seminar. Increased monthly regional volume 25 percent and helped to improve customer/company relations during my tenure.

Another way of constructing the work experience section is by using actual job descriptions. Job descriptions are rarely written using the proper resume language, but they do include all the information necessary to create this section of your resume. Take the description of one of the jobs you are including on your resume (if you have access to it), and turn it into an action-oriented paragraph. Below is an example of a job description followed by a version of the same description written using action words. Again, pay attention to the style of writing, as the details of your own work experience will be unique.

WORK EXPERIENCE

Public Administrator I

Responsibilities: Coordinate and direct public services to meet the needs of the nation, state, or community. Analyze problems; work with special committees and public agencies; recommend solutions to governing bodies.

Aptitudes and Skills: Ability to relate to and communicate with people; solve complex problems through analysis; plan, organize, and implement policies and programs. Knowledge of political systems; financial management; personnel administration; program evaluation; organizational theory.

WORK EXPERIENCE

Public Administrator I

Wrote pamphlets and conducted discussion groups to inform citizens of legislative processes and consumer issues. Organized and supervised 25 interviewers. Trained interviewers in effective communication skills.

Now that you have learned how to word your resume, you are ready for the next step in your quest for a winning resume: assembly and layout.

Chapter 3

Assembly and Layout

At this point, you've gathered all the necessary information for your resume, and you've rewritten it using the language necessary to impress potential employers. Your next step is to assemble these elements in a logical order and then to lay them out on the page neatly and attractively in order to achieve the desired effect: getting that interview.

Assembly

The order of the elements in a resume makes a difference in its overall effect. Obviously, you would not want to put your name and address in the middle of the resume or your special skills section at the top. You want to put the elements in an order that stresses your most important achievements, not the less pertinent information. For example, if you recently graduated from school and have no full-time work experience, you will want to list your education before you list any part-time jobs you may have held during school. On the other hand, if you have been gainfully employed for several years and currently hold an important position in your company, you will want to list your work experience ahead of your education, which has become less pertinent with time.

There are some elements that are always included in your resume and some that are optional. Following is a list of essential and optional elements:

Essential	**Optional**
Name	Job Objective
Address	Honors
Phone Number	Special Skills
Work Experience	Professional Memberships
Education	Activities
References Phrase	Certificates and Licenses
	Personal Information

Your choice of optional sections depends on your own background and employment needs. Always use information that will put you and your abilities in a favorable light. If your honors are impressive, then be sure to include them in your resume. If your activities in school demonstrate particular talents necessary for the job you are seeking, then allow space for a section on activities. Each resume is unique, just as each person is unique.

Types of Resumes

So far, our discussion about resumes has involved the most common type—the *reverse chronological* resume, in which your most recent job is listed first and so on. This is the type of resume usually preferred by human resources directors, and it is the one most frequently used. However, in some cases this style of presentation is not the most effective way to highlight your skills and accomplishments.

For someone reentering the workforce after many years or someone looking to change career fields, the *functional resume* may work best. This type of resume focuses more on achievement and less on the sequence of your work history. In the functional resume, your experience is presented by what you have accomplished and the skills you have developed in your past work.

A functional resume can be assembled from the same information you collected for your chronological resume. The main difference lies in how you organize this information. Essentially, the work experience section becomes two sections, with your job duties and accomplishments comprising one section and your employer's name, city, state, your position, and the dates employed making up another section. The first section is placed near the top of the resume, just below the job objective section, and can be called *Accomplishments* or *Achievements*. The second section, containing the bare essentials of your employment history, should come after the accomplishments section and can be titled *Work Experience* or *Employment History*. The other sections of your resume remain the same. The work experience section is the only one affected in the functional resume. By placing the section that focuses on your achievements first, you thereby draw attention to these achievements. This puts less emphasis on who you worked for and more emphasis on what you did and what you are capable of doing.

For someone changing careers, emphasis on skills and achievements is essential. The identities of previous employers, which may be unrelated to one's new job field, need to be downplayed. The functional resume accomplishes this task. For someone reentering the workforce after many years, a functional resume is the obvious choice. If you lack full-time work experience, you will need to draw attention away from this fact and instead focus on your skills and abilities gained possibly through volunteer activities or part-time work. Education may also play a more important role in this resume.

Which type of resume is right for you will depend on your own personal circumstances. It may be helpful to create a chronological and a functional resume and then compare the two to find out which is more suitable. The sample resumes found in this book include both chronological and functional resumes. Use these resumes as guides to help you decide on the content and appearance of your own resume.

Layout

Once you have decided which elements to include in your resume and you have arranged them in an order that makes sense and emphasizes your achievements and abilities, then it is time to work on the physical layout of your resume.

There is no single appropriate layout that applies to every resume, but there are a few basic rules to follow in putting your resume on paper:

1. Leave a comfortable margin on the sides, top, and bottom of the page (usually 1 to 1½ inches).

2. Use appropriate spacing between the sections (usually 2 to 3 line spaces are adequate).

3. Be consistent in the *type* of headings you use for the different sections of your resume. For example, if you capitalize the heading EMPLOYMENT HISTORY, don't use initial capitals and underlining for a heading of equal importance, such as Education.

CHRONOLOGICAL RESUME

Franklin Wu
5391 Southward Plaza
Walnut Creek, CA 94596
(510) 555-9008

JOB OBJECTIVE:

To obtain a position as a management optician in a fast-paced retail store.

EDUCATION:

Graduated Hayward Community College, Hayward, CA in June of 1991
Graduated North Central High School, Chicago, IL in June of 1989

WORK EXPERIENCE:

1995 - present

Great Spectacles, Walnut Creek, CA
Management Optician

Valley Vision, Pleasanton, CA
Management Optician and Frame Buyer

SPECIAL SKILLS:

People person; fashion styling experience; knowledge of adjustments, repairs, and
    fittings of glasses and contact lenses.

CERTIFICATION:

American Board of Optometry Certificate

SEMINARS:

Cal-Q Optics to prepare for licensing, 1997
Opti-Fair (annual, three-day seminars)

REFERENCES:

George Jones, O.D.
Great Spectacles, (510) 555-8941

Maria Lazar, Optician
Valley Vision, (510) 555-3726

FUNCTIONAL RESUME

PATRICIA WHITE
987 West 44th Street
Cheyenne, WY 82001
(307) 555-9872

PROFESSIONAL OBJECTIVE

Opportunity to demonstrate superior managerial ability and administrative decision-making skills in a nursing home environment.

SUMMARY OF QUALIFICATIONS

- High degree of motivation
- Ability and patience to train and develop office and professional staff
- Thorough knowledge of IBM PC, Lotus 1-2-3, WordPerfect, IBM 38
- 10-key by touch
- Dictation

EDUCATION

University of Wyoming, B.A. Business
Laramie, WY

EXPERIENCE

1994 to Present - Assistant Director, Longview Manor, Cheyenne, WY
1991 to 1994 - Business Manager, Mountain Top Nursing Home, Cheyenne, WY

REFERENCES

Excellent professional and personal references

4. Always try to fit your resume onto one page. If you are having trouble fitting all your information onto one page, perhaps you are trying to say too much. Edit out any repetitive or unnecessary information or shorten descriptions of earlier jobs. Be ruthless. Maybe you've included too many optional sections.

Don't let the idea of having to tell every detail about your life get in the way of producing a resume that is simple and straightforward. The more compact your resume, the easier it will be to read and the better an impression it will make for you.

In some cases, the resume will not fit on a single page, even after extensive editing. In such cases, the resume should be printed on two pages so as not to compromise clarity or appearance. Each page of a two-page resume should be marked clearly with your name and the page number, e.g., "Judith Ramirez, page 1 of 2." The pages should then be stapled together.

Try experimenting with various layouts until you find one that looks good to you. Always show your final layout to other people and ask them what they like or dislike about it, and what impresses them most about your resume. Make sure that is what you want most to emphasize. If it isn't, you may want to consider making changes in your layout until the necessary information is emphasized. Use the sample resumes in this book to get some ideas for laying out your resume.

Putting Your Resume in Print

Your resume should be typed or printed on good quality $8^1/_2'' \times 11''$ bond paper. You want to make as good an impression as possible with your resume; therefore, quality paper is a necessity. If you have access to a word processor with a good printer, or know of someone who does, make use of it. Typewritten resumes should only be used when there are no other options available.

After you have produced a clean original, you will want to make duplicate copies of it. Usually a copy shop is your best bet for producing copies without smudges or streaks. Make sure you have the copy shop use quality bond paper for all copies of your resume. Ask for a sample copy before they run your entire order. After copies are made, check each copy for cleanliness and clarity.

Another more costly option is to have your resume typeset and printed by a printer. This will provide the most attractive resume of all.

If you anticipate needing a lot of copies of your resume, the cost of having it typeset may be justified.

Proofreading

After you have finished typing the master copy of your resume and before you go to have it copied or printed, you must thoroughly check it for typing and spelling errors. Have several people read it over just in case you may have missed an error. Misspelled words and typing mistakes will not make a good impression on a prospective employer, as they are a bad reflection on your writing ability and your attention to detail. With thorough and conscientious proofreading, these mistakes can be avoided.

The following are some rules of capitalization and punctuation that may come in handy when proofreading your resume:

RULES OF CAPITALIZATION

- Capitalize proper nouns, such as names of schools, colleges, and universities, names of companies, and brand names of products.

- Capitalize major words in the names and titles of books, tests, and articles that appear in the body of your resume.

- Capitalize words in major section headings of your resume.

- Do not capitalize words just because they seem important.

- When in doubt, consult a manual of style such as *Words Into Type* (Prentice-Hall), or *The Chicago Manual of Style* (The University of Chicago Press). Your local library can help you locate these and other reference books.

RULES OF PUNCTUATION

- Use a comma to separate words in a series.

- Use a semicolon to separate series of words that already include commas within the series.

- Use a semicolon to separate independent clauses that are not joined by a conjunction.

- Use a period to end a sentence.

- Use a colon to show that examples or details follow that will expand or amplify the preceding phrase.

- Avoid the use of dashes.

- Avoid the use of brackets.

- If you use any punctuation in an unusual way in your resume, be consistent in its use.

- Whenever you are uncertain, consult a style manual.

The Cover Letter

O nce your resume has been assembled, laid out, and printed to your satisfaction, the next step before distribution is to write your cover letter. Though there may be instances where you deliver your resume in person, usually you send it through the mail. Resumes sent through the mail always need an accompanying letter that briefly introduces you and your resume. The purpose of the cover letter is to get a potential employer to read your resume, just as the purpose of your resume is to get that same potential employer to call you for an interview.

Like your resume, your cover letter should be clean, neat, and direct. A cover letter usually includes the following information:

1. Your name and address (unless it already appears on your personal letterhead).

2. The date.

3. The name and address of the person and company to whom you are sending your resume.

4. The salutation ("Dear Mr." or "Dear Ms." followed by the person's last name, or "To Whom it May Concern" if you are answering a blind ad).

5. An opening paragraph explaining why you are writing (in response to an ad, the result of a previous meeting, at the suggestion of someone you both know) and indicating that you are interested in whatever job is being offered.

6. One or two more paragraphs that tell why you want to work for the company and what qualifications and experience you can bring to that company.

7. A final paragraph that closes the letter and requests that you be contacted for an interview.

8. The closing ("Sincerely," or "Yours truly," followed by your signature with your name typed under it).

Your cover letter, including all of the information above, should be no more than one page in length. The language used should be polite, businesslike, and to the point. Do not attempt to tell your life story in the cover letter. A long and cluttered letter will only serve to put off the reader. Remember, you only need to mention a few of your accomplishments and skills in the cover letter. The rest of your information is in your resume. Each and every achievement should not be mentioned twice. If your cover letter is a success, your resume will be read and all pertinent information reviewed by your prospective employer.

Producing the Cover Letter

Cover letters should always be individualized, since they are always written to particular individuals and companies. Never use a form letter for your cover letter. Cover letters cannot be copied or reproduced like resumes. Each one should be as personal as possible. Of course, once you have written and rewritten your first cover letter to the point where you are satisfied with it, you can use similar wording in subsequent letters.

After you have typed your cover letter on quality bond paper, proofread it as thoroughly as you did your resume. Again, spelling errors are a sure sign of carelessness, and you don't want that to be a part of your first impression on a prospective employer. Make sure to handle the letter and resume carefully to avoid any smudges, and then mail both your cover letter and resume in an appropriately sized envelope. Be sure to keep an accurate record of all the resumes you send out and the results of each mailing, either in a separate notebook or on individual index cards.

Numerous sample cover letters appear at the end of this book. Use them as models for your own cover letter or to get an idea of how cover letters are put together. Remember, every one is unique and depends on the particular circumstances of the individual writing it and the job for which he or she is applying.

Now the job of writing your resume and cover letter is complete. About a week after mailing resumes and cover letters to potential employers, you will want to contact them by telephone. Confirm that your resume arrived, and ask whether an interview might be possible. Getting your foot in the door during this call is half the battle of a job search, and a strong resume and cover letter will help you immeasurably.

Chapter 5

Sample Resumes

This chapter contains dozens of sample resumes for people pursuing a wide variety of jobs and careers.

There are many different styles of resumes in terms of graphic layout and presentation of information. These samples also represent people with varying amounts of education and experience. Model your resume after these samples. Choose one resume, or borrow elements from several different resumes to help you construct your own.

SHARYL X. WILSON

84 Saratoga Avenue   Detroit, MI 48229   (313) 555-9388

SUMMARY

Sales and Marketing Manager with proven ability to conceptualize, structure, and achieve both market and profit objectives seeks to join the sales and marketing team of Fortune 500 manufacturer.

SALES

- Initiated sales incentive program to motivate the sales force to generate new product sales.
- Increased sales of recycled paper products from $250,000 to $600,000 in the first year. Successfully built sales to more than $3,000,000 over the next five years.
- Held total responsibility for sales of copy-type papers, which represented 40% of total sales volume. Supervised six sales professionals.
- Initiated aggressive sales efforts for additional volume, allowing increased production using idle equipment, which spread costs and substantially improved profits.
- Strongly successful in developing new corporate accounts.

MANAGEMENT AND MARKETING

- Created and implemented the Neighborhood Business Strategy concentrating sales efforts to develop business close to the mill, effectively reducing costs and improving profitability.
- Changed company image from volume supplier to a dedicated quality product producer and provider of top-level customer service, a strategy that enhanced repeat business.
- Assumed newly created position, established its purpose, and made it work profitably. Established specifications, pricing, and developed marketing strategies.
- Implemented advertising campaigns with assistance from ad agencies.

EMPLOYMENT EXPERIENCE

National Sales Manager, Starnes Paper, Subsidiary of Weyerhauser, Inc., Detroit, MI, 1994 - present

Regional Sales Manager, James River, Inc., Grand Rapids, MI, 1985 - 1994

page 1 of 2

(EMPLOYMENT EXPERIENCE cont.)

Regional Sales Manager, Specialty Papers, Greenfield Paper Company, Subsidiary of James River, Inc., Grand Rapids, MI, 1982 - 1985

Sales Manager, Greenfield Paper Company, Grand Rapids, MI, 1973 - 1982

EDUCATION

M.B.A., Harvard University, Cambridge, MA, 1973

B.S., Business and Economics, University of California, Berkeley, 1971

REFERENCES AVAILABLE UPON REQUEST

YOSHIDO UMEKI   9783 Ridgeway Drive, Evanston, IL 60204   (847) 555-2983

OBJECTIVE

A position as Publicist for a Midwest corporation

SUMMARY OF QUALIFICATIONS

- Excellent public relations skills
- Experienced and published writer
- Accustomed to working on deadline
- Flexible and hardworking
- Knowledgeable about local government, business, and community

HISTORY OF EMPLOYMENT

News Reporter, *Chicago Tribune*, 1995 - present

Specialize in local news. Complete assignments and research leads for newsworthy stories. Interview local government officials, corporate officers, community activists, and business owners. Developed the series "On Your Block" for the weekend edition, featuring various local communities. Developed a five-part story exploring community relations of Illinois corporate businesses.

Education Reporter, *Honolulu Star Bulletin*, 1989 - 1995

Started as a proofreader, within a year had written several feature stories, and within two years obtained responsibility for reporting and researching all education news.

SELECTED LIST OF PUBLICATIONS

- *Hadley and Hadley's Scramble for Community Support*
- *Community Coalition: A Homegrown Response to Woes*
- *Volunteerism: A Way of Life at Wright Brothers*
- *Hawaii's Schools: Rebuilding Promises*
- *Amelia Hunani: A New Breed of Administrator*
- *Tea and Crumpets in the Southeast District*
- *Evanston's Four-story Community: A Look at North Broadway*
- *WESTAR's Model Community Enrichment Program*

EDUCATION

Bachelor of Arts, Journalism and Government, University of Hawaii at Manoa, Honolulu

REFERENCES AND PUBLICATION PORTFOLIO ON REQUEST

Tanya Stewart
325 Matney Street
West Village, Utah 84872
(801) 555-7151

Career Objective   To bring my extensive communications background to the public relations department of a mid-sized West Coast computer company.

Related Skills   Developed and produced a prototype newsletter to be distributed
and Experience   among alumni of the College of Science at Brigham Young University. Conducted reader survey to determine market interest and gather information relevant to the publication. Supervised continued publication of the newsletter. Responded to queries from readers.

Conducted seminars on writing for publication for scientists and other technical professionals.

Designed and instituted courses in technical writing and communication for science and engineering majors.

Managed all institutional correspondence and communication with the news media.

Worked closely with public relations office of the university in developing news stories about scientific work conducted by university faculty in my college.

Widely published in scientific and technical journals. Published two textbooks on scientific method in computer-aided investigation.

Worked with science correspondents of major medical journals on the reporting of significant developments in cancer research at a medical laboratory under my direct supervision.

page 1 of 2

Employment   Brigham Young University, Provo, Utah
                  Associate Dean, College of Science, 1995 to present
                  Professor of Science, 1990 to present
                  Associate Professor, 1987 to 1990
                  Assistant Professor, 1984 to 1987

                  Mentor Laboratories, Salt Lake City, Utah
                  Director of Research, 1979 to 1984
                  Research Scientist, 1973 to 1975

Education   Bethlehem Children's Hospital, Pleasantville, Maryland
                  Postdoctoral Fellow, Cancer Research Unit, 1982 to 1984
                  Doctorate, Chemistry, University of Wisconsin, Milwaukee, 1978
                  Bachelor of Science, Chemistry, University of Miami, Florida, 1975

                  Publications list and references are available on request.

Judd Riley, Jr.
P.O. Box 1254
Sioux Falls, SD 57103
(605) 555-3828

Job Objective

Customer Service Department managerial position

Experience & Achievements

Public Relations (current)

Direct interaction with clients and the public. Assess needs and provide solutions to customer complaints. Assist in product inquiries and setting up discounting programs for qualified customers. Represent company at trade shows. Utilize strong product knowledge in handling customer complaints through analysis and evaluation of complaint report. Support for sales force and on-site technicians.

Sales & Marketing (previous)

Assisted marketing research projects and conducted a general management survey for mini-warehouse industry. Coordinated promotional campaigns, utilizing database analysis to focus on target market. Responsible for selecting, ordering, and promoting the sales of sportswear to achieve over $125,000 in sales over a six-month period. Demonstrated skills in leadership, organization, and group motivation. Supervised sales staff of fourteen. Sold custom-made sportswear. Examined and evaluated markets through on-site observations and informal interviews. Supervised employees.

Employment History

Assistant Director, Public Relations
Morris Brothers, Sioux Falls, SD, 1997 - present

Management/Marketing Assistant
S.D. Management Services, Inc., Sioux Falls, SD, 1989 - 1997

Promotion Coordinator/Sales Representative
Athletics West, Sioux Falls, SD, 1986 - 1989

Associate Sales Manager
Danken Jewelers, Sioux Falls, SD, 1983 - 1985

Education

B.A., 1983 Business and Marketing, University of Vermont, Burlington

References

Will be forwarded on request

Darius G. W. Harms
3485 Plainfield Road
Lincoln, Nebraska 68573
(402) 555-9287/gwharms@aol.com

Career Goal: A position in engineering management in the public sector

Achievements & Experience

- Supported construction and operating personnel during installation, start-up, and testing of propulsion generator and hydraulic machinery.
- Performed facility survey, prepared technical reports, and provided engineering support during construction, start-up, and testing of the propulsion turbine plant.
- Directed structural and mechanical equipment development and operations.
- Coordinated fabrication and installation of full-size mock-up for integrated sub-base turbo generator.
- Provided support to designers, draftsmen, and construction personnel to ensure compliance with technical specifications and code requirements.
- Designed various mechanical and fluid systems and assisted in procurement, installation, and testing of systems and equipment.
- Designed and assisted in construction and testing of a flow-through crude-oil handling system on oil recycler, reducing initial cost and increasing operational efficiency.
- Conducted equipment and system test at the factory and after-site installation of various recycling components, including pumps, heat exchangers, hydraulics, and control/monitoring devices.
- Assisted in installation and testing of bulk petrochemical heating system.
- Assisted during installation, start-up, and testing of machinery for fiber, film cellulose, bulk material, and processing equipment.
- Developed and assisted in installation of automated overhead conveying system to replace manual material handling operation for cellulose sheet.
- Supervised installation of the filing line to increase bagging output for micro crystalline cellulose.
- Redesigned the PVC blown film machine and provided assistance during installation and start-up. Supervised a workforce of 120 with responsibility over production and maintenance of oxygen and acetylene plant and facilities.
- Conducted the economic analysis for relocating oxygen plant. Supervised erection of the plant at the new site.

(Achievements & Experience continued)

- Designed and assisted in the fabrication of the filtering system for acetyl. Supervised start-up and testing of the system.
- Developed the test procedure for high pressure cylinders to meet regulatory requirements.

Work History

1995 - Present	Benton Recycling Machinery, Inc., Lincoln, Nebraska *Senior Engineer*
1984 - 1995	Taber Manufacturing, Lincoln, Nebraska *Engineering Supervisor*
1970 - 1979	Tutwiller Bond Oxygen Corp., Ltd., Topeka, Kansas *Staff Engineer, Maintenance Engineer, Technician*
Education	M.S., Mechanical Engineering, 1976, University of Kansas B.S., Mechanical Engineering, 1970, University of Nebraska - Lincoln

References on Request

Dr. Marvin A. Robinson

Office: (205) 555-3928   Home: (205) 555-3346
44 Buck Drive   89 Fairview Place
Huntsville, Alabama 35804   Huntsville, Alabama 35804

OBJECTIVE
A managerial position with state government in which I may put my experience and skills
in administration to best use.

EDUCATION
Ph.D., University of Iowa, School Administration, 1985
M.S., Louisiana State University, Baton Rouge, Secondary Education, 1976
B.S., Louisiana State University, Elementary Education, 1974

EMPLOYMENT
Superintendent, Huntsville Schools, Alabama, 1998 - present
Superintendent, Park School District, Prattsville, Alabama, 1990 - 1997
Principal, Mission High School, Montgomery, Alabama, 1985 - 1990
Principal, Jackson Heights Public School, Jackson, Alabama, 1983 - 1985
Assistant Principal, Jackson High School, Jackson, Alabama, 1980 - 1983
Math Teacher, Hopewell High School, Mobile, Alabama, 1976 - 1980

SELECTED AFFILIATIONS
Alabama Association of School Administrators
American Association of School Administrators
State Superintendent's Advisory Committee
State Department Evaluation Committee
Chamber of Commerce
Jobs Plus, Board of Directors
Leadership Development Program, Huntsville School District and University of Alabama
Louisiana State University, Graduate Instructor
University of Alabama, Graduate Instructor

SPEAKING ENGAGEMENTS AND CONSULTING PROJECTS
Baton Rouge, Louisiana, National Association of Secondary School Principals, "A Climate
    for Learning"
Toronto, Ontario, National Association of Secondary School Principals, "The School
    Administrator Under Stress"
National Academy for School Executives, Keynote Speaker, "Educational Accountability:
    Three Approaches"

PUBLICATIONS
"The Road to Being a Superintendent," NASSP Bulletin 34, vol 2
"Looking to the Future in American Education," ERIC
"Educational Approaches in African American Schools," Alabama Department of Education, newsletter, November 1998

HONORS
Talladega College, Member, Board of Trustees
Huntsville Chamber of Commerce, Outstanding Educator Award, 1987
Louisiana State University, President, African American Student Union
Who's Who in American Colleges and Universities

References available on request

LANE TYLER
1892 Red River Road   **Toledo, Ohio 43601**   **(419) 555-2078**

Objective   A position as Instructor of Business and Marketing

Education

M.B.A., 1997, Ohio University, Athens
B.A., 1974, State University of New York at Buffalo

Experience

1993 - present   ***Director of Marketing, Business Unit Leader, Foodservice, Pillar Paper Company, Toledo, Ohio***

Responsibilities: Strategic and marketing leadership with profit and loss accountability for a $310 million commercial foodservice business. Develop a competitively advantaged business by providing distinctive marketing, products, and services that support customer and operator needs. Direct development of environmental strategies for paper products. Provide manufacturing with objectives and standards for raw material, sourcing, quality improvement, and cost reduction. Lead business planning process.

Accomplishments: Increased division earnings by 17 percent in 1994. Initiated a new products development program. Introduced operator-focused marketing programs to pull product through distribution.

1991 - 1993   ***Senior Marketing Manager, Commercial Products Division, Pillar Paper Company, Toledo, Ohio***

Responsibilities: Led development and marketing of new high performance products and systems for towels and soaps. Developed and led a foodservice venture for the Commercial Products Division. Managed integration efforts with the Foodservice Corporation. With sales management, developed target market strategies.

Accomplishments: Led development and marketing of a new towel brand which contributed over $1 million in new earnings within eighteen months. The foodservice venture generated $2 million incremental earnings in 1993. Awarded one of three Business Excellence awards for my contributions in 1992 - 1993.

1989 - 1991   ***Senior Marketing Manager, Foodservice Division, Pillar Paper Company, Toledo, Ohio***

Responsibilities: Directed marketing and development for 650 foodservice products. Developed foodservice strategies that aligned with commercial towel and tissue business objectives. Directed Marketing Communications programs.

p. 1 of 2

Experience (cont.)

Accomplishments: Improved Specialty Products earnings by 10 percent in 1989 and 1990 with a balance of marketing programs and price guideline development.

1986 - 1989   ***Director of Marketing and Sales, American Convenience, Inc., Toledo, Ohio***

Responsibilities: Reported to the president and directed all sales and marketing functions, with accountability for continuous earnings and improvement. Responsible for product and program development, advertising, customer service, and a twenty-five person sales staff.

Accomplishments: Initiated a national accounts program. Introduced American's first sales incentive program which helped drive a 12 percent increase in sales and profits in the first year.

1981 - 1986   ***Group Products Manager, American Convenience, Inc., Toledo, Ohio***

Responsibilities: Accountable for management of all product lines toward profitable growth. Managed promotion, product design, advertising, forecasting, and pricing. Planned all national and regional trade show representation.

Accomplishments: Led development of Spectrum Colors promotional program, which significantly altered the way the industry markets color napkins.

1975 - 1981   ***Branch Sales Manager, Time-Life Books, Pittsburgh, Pennsylvania***

Responsibilities: Staffed, organized, and managed the first branch sales office in the Eastern U.S. Developed and managed testing for retail distribution of our products.

Accomplishments: Developed sales training manual for all branches. Initiated WATS line concept of national selling and reduction of sales costs.

References Provided on Request

Jerold M. Short
3554 Front Street #306
Gallup, New Mexico 87321
(505) 555-2283

Career Ambition

Teaching and research position with a major medical center or hospital.

Related Experience

Good Samaritan Hospital
Gallup, New Mexico
Emergency Room Registered Nurse
(January 1990 to present)

- Trained new emergency room nurses and technicians with appropriate ER procedures
- Triaged all incoming patients and worked with EMT staff to stabilize patients
- Assisted physicians with suturing and casting
- Administered IVs and medications
- Provided emergency medical care, including CPR
- Supervised nursing staff of emergency room during night and weekend shifts

Central Albuquerque Community Hospital
Albuquerque, New Mexico
ICU/CCU Registered Nurse
(January 1987 to November 1989)

- Supervised nursing staff on weekends
- Coordinated nursing and lay teams in providing emotional and psychological support for terminal patients and their families
- Monitored temporary pacemakers; assisted with insertion of intra-aortic balloon pumps; interpreted 12-lead electrocardiograms; inserted catheters and IVs; assisted doctors with examinations and administered required medications; assisted with cardioversions
- Instructed outpatients recovering from open-heart surgery and myocardial infarction

Related Experience - continued

Buck Ambulance
Albuquerque, New Mexico
Emergency Medical Technician
(September 1982 to January 1985)

- Responded to emergency calls for medical assistance
- Triaged patients on site and prepared for transportation to hospital or medical center facilities
- Assisted hospital medical personnel in transfer of patients and emergency room care
- Administered IVs and various types of emergency medical intervention

Education

RN, University of Santa Fe, New Mexico, 1987
EMT, University of Santa Fe, New Mexico, 1981

Memberships

Sigma Theta Tau (national honor society for nursing)
American Association of Critical Care Nurses
National Hospice Nurses Association
American Heart Association, volunteer instructor
American Red Cross, volunteer instructor

References available on request

KEVIN FOXWORTH
2114 Renton Street   Kirkland, Washington 98005   (206) 555-3497

CAREER OBJECTIVE   Engineering position with industrial manufacturing company.

CAPABILITIES

- Manage continuous fire furnaces that produce flat pressed glass and glass for machine and hand blowing.

- Plan and supervise all aspects of furnace operation and maintenance, including personnel scheduling and staffing.

- Evaluate alternative production methods and materials to reduce costs and improve product quality.

- Control raw materials inventory, ordering, and inspection.

- Train employees in use and maintenance of equipment.

- Review product availability and equipment developments to keep systems up-to-date for both production and safety concerns.

- Plan, coordinate, and supervise all aspects of glassware production.

ACHIEVEMENTS

- Initiated improved method for raw materials handling that resulted in $250,000 in actual savings.

- Worked with production engineers to develop new heating procedures that made furnaces 20 percent more efficient in start-up time.

- Developed operating procedures that improved worker safety.

- Designed alternative casting that reduced external temperatures dramatically, thus decreasing fire and burn hazard.

- Given Award of Merit for developing material composition that produced greater clarity in present glass products.

WORK HISTORY

1985 - present	Pihuck GlassWorks Factory, Kirkland, Washington Furnace/Production Manager
1974 - 1985	Boeing, Renton, Washington Senior Technician, Instrumentation Casing Section

EDUCATION

1998	B.S., Engineering, University of Washington
1973	A.A., Technology and Industry Production, Everett Community College, Everett, Washington

REFERENCES   Available when requested

DAVID SAMUELS
84 BAYONETT STREET
CHATTANOOGA, TENNESSEE 34701
(615) 555-9388

SUMMARY:

Sales and marketing manager who wishes to enter the publishing industry as sales representative or sales manager. Proven leadership ability to conceptualize, structure, and achieve both market and profit objectives.

PROFESSIONAL EXPERIENCE:

National Sales Manager, Washington Paper, Subsidiary of PaperGraphics, Inc., Chattanooga, TN, 1994 - Present
- Assumed total responsibility for sales of commodity and specialty papers in the United States and Canada with total sales in excess of $50 million.
- Coordinated with manufacturing the transfer of specialty paper manufacturing to another mill. Upgraded that mill from commodity to specialty paper producer.
- Created and implemented the Neighborhood Business Strategy, concentrating sales efforts to develop business close to the mill, effectively reducing costs and improving profit sales incentive program to motivate the sales force to generate new product sales.
- Initiated aggressive sales efforts for additional volume, allowing increased production, using idle equipment, which spread costs and substantially improved profits.

Sales Manager, Repro-paper, Inc., Subsidiary of PaperGraphics, Inc., Buffalo, NY, 1985 - 1994
- Managed sales of all copy-type papers, which represented 40 percent of sales.
- Directed department of six sales professionals.
- Reduced dependence on major accounts by expanding customer base and raising prices.
- Improved profitability stressing quality, service, and elimination of volume price contracts, which were depressing profits.
- Changed company image perception from volume supplier to top-quality product producer dedicated to customer service.
- Supported our customers through National Trade and Industry Association participation.

Product Manager, Specialty Papers, Greenfield Paper Company, Subsidiary of PaperGraphics, Inc., Greenfield, MA, 1982 - 1985
- Assumed newly created position, established its function, and made it work profitably.
- Established specifications and pricing and developed marketing strategies.
- Consolidated product lines in greeting card, wallpaper, photographic, and flameproof markets.
- Developed trade names, product identification, and customer recognition.
- Implemented advertising campaigns with assistance from ad agencies.
- Worked with technical department to develop technical bulletins and supporting materials in the greeting card, wallpaper, photographic, and flameproof markets.
- Worked closely with regional salesmen and their customers to develop greater product use and customer satisfaction.

page 1 of 2

(PROFESSIONAL EXPERIENCE *continued*)

Salesperson, Greenfield Paper Company, 1973 - 1982
- Increased sales from $250,000 to $600,000 in the first year.
- Successfully built sales to more than $3,000,000 by 1982.
- Recognized as especially proficient in developing new sales leads.

EDUCATION:

B.S., Business, University of Pittsburgh, Pennsylvania, 1973

AFFILIATIONS:

American Marketing Association
Chattanooga Business Alliance
Chattanooga Chamber of Commerce

HONORS:

Excellence in Marketing Award, AMA, 1985
Mayor's Certificate of Service, 1992
Businessperson of the Year, 1993

REFERENCES:

Available upon request

LUCILLE SIRIOS

392 Alturn Drive, Geneva, Illinois 60134
Home (815) 555-8372/Work (312) 555-3846

OBJECTIVE

Advertising staff of a major international publishing house. Particularly interested in a position that will utilize my written and verbal fluency in German.

PROFESSIONAL EXPERIENCE

Berlin American, Chicago, IL, Manager and Buyer, 1993 - present
- Develop, produce and implement direct main and newspaper advertising campaigns that have directly contributed to a 45% sales growth over four years.
- Buy and merchandise German textile and ceramic handcrafted items.
- Maintain financial control of $375,000 annual sales volume.
- Translate business-related documents, German/English and English/German.

Books, Etc., Bookstore, Minneapolis, MN, Manager/Regional Planner, 1989 - 1993
- Responsible for effective visual presentation for three area stores.
- Trained and supervised ten employees.
- Controlled inventory and financial planning of $300,000 annual sales volume.

La France, Edina, MN, Counter Manager, 1985 - 1989
- Supervised staff of twelve waiters.
- Supervised food preparation and distribution.
- Integrated daily cash receipts into restaurant financial budget.
- Wrote and engineered news programming and public service announcements.

EDUCATION

St. John's University, Collegeville, MN

Bachelor of Arts in Government and German, awarded June 1989

Institutes for American Universities, Berlin, Germany

German language coursework, 1993

References Available

FAITH NGUYEN   775 S. W. Tillbury Road, Fresno, CA 93723   (203) 555-7623

CAREER OBJECTIVE: Project Management Director

EXPERIENCE:

Communications Manager, Consortium of California Counties, Fresno,
1993 - present

The Consortium administers an annual federal grant of $25 million for employment and training programs in 35 counties. As the first Communications Manager of the Administrative Office, I developed and implemented a public relations effort for the Job Training Partnership Act (JTPA).

Highlights:

- Develop annual report, newsletter, brochures, and other materials to market program's job training services to private business, public sector, and job seekers.
- Received National Business Alliance Distinguished Performance Award.
- Conceived and managed a statewide conference for employment and training professionals; hosted visiting International Fellowship representatives from four European countries.
- Directed work of advertising agency and support staff.
- Coordinated communications among various branches and county officers.
- Designed and maintained systems for recruiting, selecting, and training members of the Private Industry Association of California and local elected officials of the CCC Board of Directors. Managed quarterly meetings and biannual retreat.
- Supervised effort to diversify funding resources for the CCC.
- Coordinated multimedia job seeker recruitment campaign used in 26 states.
- Responsible for tracking state and federal legislation with potential impact on CCC programs. Prepared testimony and information for legislators. Attended state legislative hearings.

Risk Manager, Consortium of California Counties, Fresno, 1991 - 1993

Developed and implemented risk management system to assure limitation of program risks and compliance with federal and state laws. Served as liaison to district branch offices and state, regional, and federal offices of the Department of Labor in the interpretation and implementation of laws and regulations.

Highlights:

- Developed system of procedures to identify and monitor program risks.
- Conducted comprehensive Risk Management Reviews of district for compliance with state and federal laws.

page 1 of 2

EXPERIENCE (cont.):

- Responsible for development, training, and implementation of EEO/AA policy and Affirmative Action Plan. Investigated and processed complaints.
- Developed grievance procedure and trained all CCC managers statewide.

Personnel Director, International Paper Suppliers, San Francisco, CA, 1982 - 1986

Responsible for Industrial Relations functions and monitoring of EEO/AA activities for corporation with 95 corporate locations nationwide. First woman in the corporation's history to hold this position. (Hired in Corporate Communications Department in 1978.)

Highlights:

- Interpreted and administered labor contract and represented the company in local and master bargaining.
- Developed corporate policy manual on EEO/AA. Designed a brochure for corporate use and conducted regional EEO/AA seminars in corporate supervisory training courses.
- Coordinated corporate community programs.
- Worked with field managers to prepare for government regulations compliance review.

EDUCATION:

B.A. in Communications, Stanford University, CA, 1978

Portfolio and references available upon request

JOSEPH W. CALDWELL

346 Buena Vista
Pocatello, Idaho 83251
(208) 555-6682 or E-mail: aol@buildit.com

Job Goal:

Construction foreman for housing construction company.

Skills:

Experienced in a wide range of construction and wood products occupations.

Thorough knowledge of indigenous woods and their suitability for construction.

Twenty years of supervisory experience.

Work History:

Supervisor, Twin Peaks Plywood, Pocatello, ID

Trained and supervised mill workers in all areas of mill operation. Scheduled shifts of 24 workers each, three shifts a day. Worked relief schedule on weekends. Developed safety awareness program. Monitored safety procedures. Consulted with SAIF inspectors for methods of improving working environment safety. Employed continuously from 1988 to present.

Shift Foreman, Idaho Lumber Supply, Boise, ID

Supervised splitters, pullers, and saw operators on day shift. Trained workers in all aspects of lumber mill operation. Monitored safety procedures. Employed initially as mill worker; worked seasonally from 1982 to 1988 (moved).

Carpentry Crewman, Dales Construction, Boise, ID

Worked on carpentry crew building residential dwellings and office complexes in Boise and environs. Experienced with foundation work, roofing, sheet-rocking, and finish carpentry. Worked seasonally from 1979 to 1988 (moved).

Woodworker, Ames Oak Furniture, Boise, ID

Operated lathe, power saw, miter saw, drill press, scroll saw, burnishing sander, and other power equipment in the manufacture and finishing of oak furniture. Employed full-time from 1977 to 1979 (business relocated out of state).

Education:

Boise Central High School, graduated 1977

Memberships:

International Mill Workers Local #655; Carpenters Local #2815

Janet Lee Kosh
2314 Sunnyview Drive, N.W.
Springfield, Missouri 65812
(417) 555-9076

Professional Objective:

Seeking new challenges in a position as communications director in a private-sector corporate environment.

Previous Experience:

Director of Communications, City of Springfield, MO, October 1991 to present

- *Plan and direct* public information program for the City of Springfield.

- *Supervise* city management communications with the general public and corporate representatives.

- *Coordinate* writing, design, and production of city's annual report to taxpayers, newsletter to local businesses and the chamber of commerce members, and brochures covering important aspects of city planning.

- *Consult* with business leaders, civic leaders, and public arts organizations on fundraising programs for community-wide projects.

Director of Communications, Office of Development, Washington University, St. Louis, MO, 1983 to 1990

- *Plan* communications strategies and programs for corporate, individual, and alumni fundraising efforts.

- *Direct* public information program: write and distribute press releases and feature articles, coordinate and secure necessary design services, plan and develop new public information and publication projects as needs are identified.

- *Respond* to information requests from the general public, university faculty and students, and alumni.

- *Coordinate* inter-departmental fundraising tracking system and communications.

Publications Coordinator, Cartwright/Haeuser/Martinez Architects, St. Louis, MO, 1978 to 1983

- *Write, edit, and submit* articles to professional and trade journals; prepare entries for architectural awards programs.

- *Maintain* project books and photo and slide files for use in client presentations.

- *Develop* presentation graphics; *contract* with designers.

- *Produce* general office graphic materials, including 240-page bound promotional book.

page 1 of 2

Honors & Awards:

Gold Award, Two-Color Publications, CASE National, 1983
Silver Award, One-Color Publications, CASE National, 1982
Gold Award, Capital Campaign, CASE National, 1982

Education:

Bachelor of Arts, Graphic Design/Writing (dual major), Washington University, 1975

Continuing Education Conferences & Workshops:

Design and Communications for Corporate Publications, Dallas, Texas, 1993
City Manager's Association Conference, annually, 1991 - present
Getting Things Done, CareerTrack Seminar, Vancouver, B.C., Canada, 1991
Desktop Publishing Seminar, Publish Magazine, San Francisco, California, 1990
CASE Conference on Capital Campaign Communications, Indianapolis, Indiana, 1990

References and portfolio furnished upon request

NORTON W. WALTERS

10563 S.E. Powell Blvd., Tulsa, Oklahoma 75135 (918) 555-4436

PERSONAL FOCUS

Financial analysis and strategic marketing management

PROFESSIONAL EXPERIENCE

Financial

Financial analysis, cash flow analysis, securities analysis, business and economic forecasting and feasibility studies.

Marketing

Market analysis and testing, strategic planning and administration, market research, opinion polling and analysis, coordinating and facilitating focus groups.

Management

Program and project management, staff supervision, budget preparation and administration, MIS reviews and management audits, public relations, staff development, personnel recruitment and selection, union contract interpretation and administration, Affirmative Action and EEO compliance planning and administration.

Communication

Team building, employee relations counseling, dispute resolution and mediation, public speaking, report writing, group facilitation.

CAREER PATH

President and CEO, Step One Enterprises, 1994 - present

Began and manage trading and brokerage corporation with affiliations in China, Hong Kong, Taiwan, and the Philippines. Sold business after achieving personal and professional goals.

Consultant, Various corporate and public sector clients, 1991 - 1994

Provided business consulting services in market analysis, marketing strategy and planning, public relations, budgeting and financial analysis.

CAREER PATH CONTINUED

Division Manager, State of Oklahoma, Employment and Human Services,
1980 - 1990

Managed job development and placement with staff of 24. Conducted program evaluation and planning. Developed public relations program and hired personnel. Served as liaison to Governor's office for employment issues.

EDUCATION

Master of Business Administration, Finance and Management
University of California, Berkeley, 1990

Bachelor of Arts, Philosophy
University of Colorado, Boulder, 1966

References furnished upon request

JANE P. HARPER
8395 Beaumont Drive
Lincoln, Nebraska 68508

OBJECTIVE: A managerial position in a major Midwest private corporation that will maximize my proven abilities in:

- Administrative Management
- Organizational Development
- Corporate Affairs
- Public and Community Relations

SKILLS/EXPERIENCE

- Recruited, trained, and developed management teams of up to 15, supervising up to 2,800 employees.
- Successfully prepared and administered operating and capital budgets totaling up to $133 million.
- Experienced in initiating and overseeing all operating functions associated with capital improvement projects totaling $150 million.
- Developed marketing and public relations programs that generated significant private-sector business. Created public and private-sector partnerships that fostered substantial commercial and entrepreneurial growth.
- Guided operations analyses resulting in significant efficiency improvements and cost savings through changes in work processes and operating procedures, upgrades to management methods and systems, and reallocation and downsizing of workforce.

CAREER HISTORY

Chief Executive Officer, City of Lincoln, NE

- Recruited in 1996 to improve the financial situation, strengthen organizational planning and development as well as establish better communication and information management systems. Responsible for administrative and business affairs including management staffing, budgeting, finance, employee relations, service programs, and community relations.
- Initiated multilevel operations analysis used as basis for creating new strategic plan.

CAREER HISTORY continued

- Identified and led planning, design, and completion of capital improvement projects totaling more than $150 million.
- Supervised development of business plan that reduced operating costs $800,000 in key corporate component.
- Initiated analysis and guided development of internal organization to better manage labor relations and employee benefits functions. Eliminated two-year backlog of unresolved worker compensation cases.
- Prepared and implemented reorganization that resulted in creation of central data processing and management information services functions.
- Led and implemented reorganization that resulted in creation of central data processing and management information services functions.

General Manager, City of Greeley, Colorado

- Recruited in 1994 to unify and upgrade administrative systems/procedures and gain better control of finances. Responsible for all day-to-day operations.
- Introduced coordinated management reporting system which yielded significant improvements in internal/external communications, management decision making, and organizational efficiency.
- Adapted existing budget to modified zero-base budgeting system.
- Reversed trend of economic base erosion by working with existing businesses to foster expansion and improved competitiveness.

Previous Experience: Includes progressive general management positions in public sector organizations in Florida, Oklahoma, and Maine.

EDUCATION

Master's Degree, Marcus Graduate School, University of Ohio, Athens, 1990
Bachelor's Degree, Bates College, Lewiston, Maine, 1985

References provided on request

ADRIAN KASIMOR
389 NORTH BEND
IOWA CITY, IOWA 52240
(319) 555-2243

OBJECTIVE:

A position involved in the management of a conference center or conference services

EXPERIENCE:

Assistant Director, Iowa Summer Quarter, 1990 - present, University of Iowa, Iowa City
- Direct administrative operations, University of Iowa Summer Quarter.
- Make policy decisions and direct long-range planning.
- Responsible for program development and communications with vice-presidents, academic deans, department chairs, and academic unit personnel.
- Manage the development, preparation, justification of budgets and accounting operations.
- Direct marketing and publicity campaign.

Conference Administrator, 1985 - 1990, University of Iowa, Iowa City
- Managed biannual international seminars.
- Produced brochures, made registration and site arrangements, developed and maintained operating budget.
- Coordinated additional conferences, seminars, workshops.

Administrative Assistant, 1982 - 1985, University of Iowa, Iowa City
- Managed/supervised Academic Records Department.
- Assisted in start-up operations of University Conference and Performing Arts Center.

EDUCATION:

University of Iowa, Iowa City

B.A., Psychology, 1981

OTHER COURSES AND WORKSHOPS:

- Supervision
- WordPerfect Desktop Publishing
- The New Supervisor/Manager
- Practical Ways to Improve Your Communication

REFERENCES:

Available on request

Tucker Wendell
P.O. Box 12597
Cincinnati, Ohio 45204
(513) 555-9041

Objective

To continue my work with young people in a position as a vocational counselor in a program involved with at-risk or disadvantaged youth.

Experience	Skills
Hired and trained workers in a variety of positions with a food-processing company.	Ability to work well with a wide range of people. Knowledge of job training and hiring procedures.
Supervised high school-age workers in fast food restaurant.	Understanding of work requirements and skills of teenage workers.
Served as volunteer coordinator of annual jobs fair for high school students. Worked with business people, professionals, and employers to develop program directed to high school students for career planning and preparation.	Developed understanding of employer needs and expectations in local job market. Ability to counsel students on job demands and opportunities. Developed contacts in the work world that could be invaluable to young people seeking job opportunities.
Assisted with summer camp and outdoor school programs for local school district. Taught woodworking segment at camp.	Ability to work with children of all ages, from elementary student campers to the high school students who worked as camp counselors.
Served as president of the Parent-Teacher Association.	Ability to work with parents to solve problems.

Employment History

Employment and Training Manager, Food-Pac Corporation, Cincinnati, Ohio   1995 - present

Responsible for hiring and training line workers and shift supervisors in food-processing company. Work with local employment agencies and high school and college counselors to find qualified individuals for specialty assignments. Handle employee performance evaluations. Developed reporting system to monitor productivity and established reward program.

Manager, Burger King Corporation, Store #1252   1985 - 1995

Hired and trained high school students and older workers for food preparation and cashier positions. Monitored sales reports. Scheduled shifts. Conducted employee performance reviews.

Education

Parker Community College, Cincinnati, A.A. in Business, 1995

References available upon request

Joella Baker   3932 North Vista, Tucson, Arizona 85726   (602) 555-3828

Objective

A position in public relations or promotion that will require my organizational, communications, and planning skills.

Professional Experience

Office Manager, Health Consortium, Tucson, AZ, 1995 - present
Organize and direct all company office activities including interviewing, selecting, training, scheduling, and supervising office support personnel; oversee administration of employee benefits plans and assisting with claims. Assist in compliance to Arizona Safety Board reporting regulations.

Establish effective procedures and policies; oversee quality performance of customer service, public relations, and clerical activities; trouble shoot complex and/or sensitive customer problems. Plan work flow assignments to successfully meet all established deadlines and management objectives; interact effectively with all departments to provide highest levels of efficiency and to maintain excellent standards of customer service.

Assist controller with cash management and other financial duties. Assist in banking negotiations and procedures pertinent to Chapter 11 status.

- Proficient in use of IBM and compatible ACCPAC accounting and word processing systems and software.

Credit & Collection Manager, Health Consortium, Tucson, AZ, 1991 - 1995
Responsible for reviewing and verifying company credit applications and setting credit limits for clients. Developed and recommended appropriate changes in credit policy to management. Processed authorized orders, prepared invoices; credited account payments and tracked past due amounts. Sent late notices and negotiated customer payment arrangements for collection of delinquent account balances.

Customer Service Manager, Health Consortium, Tucson, AZ, 1985 - 1991
Made direct contact with customers and prospective clients; maintained highest possible customer service standards. Maintained current knowledge of sales and special promotional events; served as support and backup for marketing/sales force. Provided customers with general and technical product information and special assistance. Promptly resolved order and/or account problems; ensured that orders were received; interacted effectively with other company departments; tracked order shipments through contact with freight company representatives.

Page 1 of 2

Professional Experience cont.

Conducted customer research projects to determine amendments and/or new, improved features and service policies.

- Selected to represent Health Consortium at key trade shows.
- Promoted to Credit and Collection Manager.

Receptionist/Cost Accounting, Penobscot Wire & Cable, Everett, MA 1983 - 1985
Answered and directed incoming/outgoing switchboard calls; verified job cost information; performed daily calculations and maintained accurate and current bookkeeping records; responsible for miscellaneous clerical assignments.

Sales/Office Support Staff, Brunswick River News, Everett, MA, 1980 - 1983
Developed major promotional ideas for increasing print advertising revenues; coordinated sales of regular block and classified advertising sections. Served as personal liaison to advertising agencies in the Everett and Boston areas; made effective sales presentations and secured new accounts.
Maintained accounts receivable; made bank deposits; performed billing functions. Assisted controller with collections activities and served as office receptionist.

- Established successful two-page advertising section for Before School promotion; initiated Drive Slow feature and New England Antique Paper advertising sections.

Education and Training

B.A. in Business Administration, University of Arizona, Tucson, AZ, 1995

References available on request

Jefferson Bird
3829 High Road
Warwick, RI 02887
(401) 555-9287

OBJECTIVE

A position in engineering in the public sector

BACKGROUND SUMMARY

Over twenty years experience in construction and mechanical engineering for private corporations, specifically: field engineer for installation of propulsion turbine plant on land-based test site; industrial and product engineering in the shipbuilding, material handling, chemical, and gas industries in construction, maintenance, engineering, and administrative capacities.

EDUCATION

M.S., Mechanical Engineering, 1975, Eastern University, Springfield, MA

B.S., Mechanical Engineering, 1971, Pennsylvania Institute of Technology, Pittsburgh, PA

EXPERIENCE

1992 - Present   Newport Shipbuilders, Inc., Warwick, RI
Senior Engineer

- Supported construction and operating personnel during installation, start-up, and testing of propulsion, generator, and hydraulic machinery.

- Performed facility survey, prepared technical reports, and provided engineering support during construction set-up, and testing of the propulsion turbine plant.

- Assisted in construction during structural and mechanical equipment support and foundation.

- Coordinated fabrication and installation of full-size mock-up for integrated sub-base turbo generator.

- Provided support to designers, draftsmen and construction personnel to ensure compliance with technical specifications and code requirements.

Page 1 of 2

EXPERIENCE cont.

1984 - 1992   Shipbuilders Corporation, Providence, RI
Engineering Supervisor

- Designed various mechanical and fluid systems and assisted in procurement, installation, and testing of systems and equipment.

- Designed and assisted in construction and testing of flow-through crude oil handling system on 120,000-ton double-hull tanker, reducing initial cost and increasing operational efficiency.

- Organized a multidisciplinary team to develop and build an oil-water separator to meet pollution control requirements.

- Conducted equipment and system test at the factory and after completion of installation for various components, including pumps, heat exchangers, hydraulics, and control/monitoring devices.

- Assisted in installation and testing of bulk petrochemical heating system to maintain the product temperature.

1980 - 1984   TEC, Fiber Division, Boston, MA
Staff Engineer

- Assisted during installation, start-up, and testing of machinery for fiber, film, cellulose, and bulk material and processing equipment.

- Developed and assisted in installation of automated overhead conveying system to replace manual material handling operation for cellulose sheet.

- Supervised installation of the filling line to increase bagging output for micro-crystalline cellulose.

- Redesigned the PVC blown film machine and provided assistance during installation and start-up.

1978 - 1980   Pennsylvania Oxygen Corp., Ltd., Pittsburgh, PA
Assistant Engineer

- Supervised workforce of 120 with responsibility over production and maintenance for oxygen and acetylene plant and facilities.

- Conducted the economic analysis for relocating oxygen plant. Supervised erection of the plant at the new site.

References on Request

STUART DAVID MARKS

66-B West 45th Street, Wilmington, Delaware 19835   (302) 555-8223

PROFESSIONAL OBJECTIVE

To bring my extensive experience as a certified accountant into the administration of a large metropolitan art museum.

EDUCATION

University of Chicago   M.B.A., 1983
Emphasis: Finance/Accounting
Illinois State University   B.S., 1978
Emphasis: Accounting

WORK EXPERIENCE

Corporate Accounting Manager, Bowles and Sharp, C.P.A., 1987 to present

- Direct staff of 27 certified public accountants and 15 support staff.
- Responsible for all corporate accounts, valued at more than $7.5 billion.
- Serve as liaison between accounting department and corporate CEOs.
- Reduced losses through implementation of cost accounting controls for two major corporate clients.
- Supervise corporate audits and hold final responsibility for federal and state reporting.
- Develop and maintain strategic corporate plans and accounting division budgets.

Certified Public Accountant, Truant Michaels & Associates, Inc., 1983 to 1987

- Handled ongoing accounting and reporting for 27 corporate clients.
- Prepared corporate and individual federal income tax reports.
- Audited corporate and public organization finances.
- Prepared financial statements for credit reporting and bank financing.

MEMBERSHIPS

Certified Public Accountants of Delaware
National Association of Certified Public Accountants

REFERENCES

Available upon request

Donna Everson
1233 Mission Street, San Pablo, California 98329
(212) 555-0812 or everson@aol.net

Goal

Obtain a sales or marketing position requiring analysis and strategic planning

Education   Oregon State University, 1998
                   M.B.A., Marketing

                   Massachusetts Institute of Technology, 1979
                   M.S., Civil Engineering

                   University of California, Los Angeles, 1977
                   B.S., Engineering

Experience   CH2M Hill, Inc.
                   1990 - 1996

Civil Engineer

- Responsible for analysis and design of transportation systems.
- Coordinated planning and construction with city, state, and federal government.
- Successfully negotiated contract for $26.8 million in highway construction for the city of Los Angeles.
- Responsible for developing cost-benefit ratios, staff and material estimates and schedules, and project budgets.
- Experienced with computer-aided design, drafting, and structural analysis.

——— ◆ ———

                   Shell Oil Company
                   1980 - 1990

Engineering Sales Specialist

- Responsible for home heating oil sales program and technical support for distribution companies.
- Designed and implemented a marketing program for potential distributors that resulted in a 23% increase in sales over the previous year.
- Developed a network of technical support for both distributors and end-users of the product.

Honors   Who's Who in Engineering, 1995
                   Chapter President, Society of Women Engineers, 1994 - 1996

References   Available on request

Deanna Smith

3476 W. Seventh   Las Vegas, NV 89133   (702) 555-4756

Career Goal: Director or Administrator position with government agency.

Achievements

- Directed administrative operations for college continuing education program.
- Made policy decision with regard to operations management and communications.
- Responsible for long-range planning and program development.
- Acted as liaison to department directors and college top administration.
- Managed development, preparation, and justification of accounting and budgeting operations.
- Coordinated annual international seminar, including registration, accommodations, travel and site arrangements, budgeting, and production of brochures.
- Supervised department of academic records.
- Coordinated conferences, seminars, and workshops with a variety of government and private organizations.
- Assisted in start-up operations of conference center.
- Experienced with corporate general ledger bookkeeping, auditing, payroll, and year-end closing.
- Experienced with credit management, credit reviews, and collections.

Employment Experience

Assistant Director, Continuing Education, University of Nevada, Las Vegas, NV, 1998 - present
Conference Center Associate Administrator, UNLV Conference Center, 1990 - present
Management Assistant, Continuing Education, UNLV, 1994 - 1998
Assistant to the Director, Continuing Education, UNLV, 1992 - 1994
Administrative Assistant, Continuing Education, UNLV, 1990 - 1992
Secretary, Continuing Education, UNLV, 1988 - 1990
Corporate Accounting, Miller & Sherwin, Engineering Associates, Las Vegas, NV, 1986 - 1988
Accounts Receivable, Caesar's Palace, Las Vegas, NV, 1982 - 1986

Education

B.A. in Business Administration, UNLV, 1998
Las Vegas Business College, Office Management, 1982

References available as requested

DAVID J. MASTERS
169 Broad Street
Concord, New Hampshire 03301
(603) 555-3948

CAREER OBJECTIVE

Marketing associate with the advertising department of a major retailer

EDUCATION

Continuing Education Coursework, Concordia College, 1997 to 1998
Business courses in marketing, management, and advertising

Bachelor of Science, Library Science, Boston University, 1971

EMPLOYMENT RECORD

Research and Development Specialist, Public Relations Department, New Hampshire Job Training Program, Concord, 1984 to present.

Provide job market consulting services, prepare program proposals and contracts, coordinate activities with consultants, and handle customer service. Complete study of present and future needs of the administrative unit and district offices, including capability of service delivery based on anticipated funding. Draft and implement a plan for research and development activities, with primary emphasis on identifying funding sources. Develop and maintain videos, training programs, and individual resources. Supervise staff of seven; serve as liaison to county offices.

Research Librarian, Business and Technology Department, County Library, Concord, New Hampshire, 1976 to 1984.

Maintained active records on resources for research in business and technology. Responded to queries from library patrons for research resources. Worked with individuals to develop research plans for using library resources. Remained current with new developments in the field. Supervised staff of five.

page 1 of 2

EMPLOYMENT RECORD continued

Associate Librarian, New Hampshire State Library
Concord, New Hampshire, 1971 to 1976.

Maintained all state, local, and federal government publications. Developed catalog of publications available at the state library facility. Supervised library interns in cataloging project for state library system.

REFERENCES

Available on request.

ALICIA CARPENTIER
3890 West Arlington, Syracuse, NY 13201 (315) 555-3294

OBJECTIVE

A position as music department director at a public high school

OVERVIEW

- Ten years as a private instrumental, voice, and music theory teacher.
- Founder and director of *Santos*, a Renaissance choral and instrumental group.
- Coordinated fundraising for the Arts Council: established goals, formulated policies, organized efforts.

RELATED ACTIVITIES

1991 - current:	Founded performance group focused on Renaissance music. Coordinated extensive research on early instrumentation, authenticity of performance. Act as director, arrange scores, and organize performances for the nonprofit chorus, *Santos*.
1996 and 1997:	Conductor of Student Orchestra, New York State Music Festival
1985 - 1991:	Member, Sacred Choir of Syracuse
1985 - 1991:	Member, Oberlin Conservatory Chorus; Member, A Cappella Choir

EDUCATION

M.A. in Renaissance Music History and Instrumentation, State University of New York, Syracuse, New York, 1987

B.A. in Musical Performance and Direction, Oberlin Conservatory of Music, Oberlin, Ohio, 1985

Page 1 of 2

EMPLOYMENT HISTORY

1995 - current   Director of Fundraising, Syracuse Community Arts Council,
                      Syracuse, NY

Develop fundraising programs. Coordinate solicitation and disbursement of funds.
Establish fundraising goals and policies for collecting contributions. Establish
relationships with local, regional, and national organizations and coordinate events,
support bases, and contacts.

1990 - 1995   Assistant Publicist, Syracuse Community Arts Council, Syracuse, NY

Wrote press releases, delivered presentations, and designed fliers and posters
announcing competitions and events. Organized community events. Coordinated the
1994 Arts in the Park celebration in downtown Syracuse.

1985 - 1995   Private Music Instructor, Syracuse, NY

Taught voice, piano, and violin lessons on an individual basis. Instructed children and
adults in basic music theory and technique.

References Provided Upon Request

EVELYN TICKEL
4987 Broadway, Boulder, Colorado 80304
303-555-3892

Objective

A position as a high school science or environmental studies teacher

Education

University of Colorado, Boulder, CO, Teaching Certification, grades 1 - 12, 1997

Colorado State University, Fort Collins, CO, Bachelor of Science, Zoology, 1972

Professional Experience

Instructor, Boulder County Environmental Education Center,
Boulder, CO

Instructed classes in zoology, environmental ecology, and plant and tree identification, using classroom and outdoor hands-on techniques. Supervised overnight trips for high school-aged students. Developed and wrote booklet on endangered Colorado wildlife for use as a textbook. Volunteer, part-time staff, 1995 - present.

Biological Assistant, University of Colorado Wildlife Department,
Boulder, CO

Participated in capture, tagging, and relocation of bighorn sheep in Colorado, and in dietary studies of large ungulates. Assisted in research of black-capped chickadees: made sonogram recordings, maintained 75 birds. Assisted in research of endangered fish species in Western Colorado rivers: collected fish, identified species, collected data, performed literature search, and compiled and condensed information. 1994 - 1995.

Consultant, Pokahu Ranch,
Maui, HI

Developed and wrote a conservation plan for the protection and restoration of the native ecosystem. Researched and evaluated the natural history, recovery plans, regulations, and recommendations of government officials. Performed species counts and determined the possibilities of rehabilitation of disturbed lands, eradication of pests, and reintroduction of endangered species. April - June 1995.

Page 1

Professional Experience (continued)

Scientific Technician, Washington State Department of Fisheries, Olympia, WA

Assisted in biological studies to assess the use of natural and artificial habitats by marine fish species for the purpose of developing criteria for habitat protection, mitigation, and enhancement. Collected and compiled data on salmons for habitat protection and harvest management protection purposes, including species identification, length, weight, scale sampling, sex, mark sampling, tagging, and red salmon spawning "nests" identification. Identified marine micro-invertebrates for fish stomach analysis. Performed herring and smelt spawn surveys, plankton tows, beach seines, and eelgrass samples. Interviewed sport and commercial fishers. Prepared data summaries, charts, illustrations, and graphs. Various departments, 1972 - 1994.

References provided upon request

MARGARET HALVORSEN
154 Shoreline Drive
Chicago, IL 60611
(312) 555-1707 home or (312) 555-3602 office

OBJECTIVE

TECHNICAL WRITING AND EDITORIAL MANAGEMENT

HIGHLIGHTS OF QUALIFICATIONS

- Researched and wrote science biographies for technical reference books.

- Developed and wrote employee training manuals, catalogs, and brochures, advertising copy, and press materials for retail businesses.

- Wrote and edited a broad range of grant proposals for technical and lay audiences.

- Developed, wrote, and designed public relations and fundraising materials.

- Strong background in word processing, desktop publishing, and graphics software on Macintosh and IBM computer platforms.

WORK EXPERIENCE

Director, Corporate & Foundation Relations, University of Chicago Office of Development, Chicago, IL, 1995 - present

Grant Writer, Fundraising & Development Office, University of Chicago Press, Chicago, IL, 1990 - 1995

Promotions Manager and Events Coordinator, Pattersen's Books, Chicago, IL, 1980 - 1985

EDUCATION

Columbia University, B.A. with Distinction, Phi Beta Kappa, English with Creative Writing Emphasis, 1980.

Additional coursework included microbiology, chemistry, calculus, geology, statistics, and computer science.

WRITING PORTFOLIO AND REFERENCES AVAILABLE

PAMELA MILES

33 Hardesty Lane, Apt. 34   Tallahassee, FL 32303   (904) 555-9283

Objective

A position as art teacher at the primary or secondary school level.

Education

Teacher's Certification for primary and secondary art instruction, 1998.

B.S., Art (Humanities and Social Sciences), Florida State University, 1977.

Qualification Highlights

- Certified to teach art in Florida.

- Experienced with teaching grade school children arts and crafts projects at Children's Activity Center.

- Knowledgeable about art media and techniques, including computer graphics.

- Experienced at planning schedules, events, and programs.

Professional Work Experience

Director of Development Communications

1986 - present, Office of Development, Florida State University, Tallahassee.

Plan and direct the public information program of the FSU Office of Development. Organize the design and production of organizational publications and plan the annual publications schedule. Gather information to write news releases and feature articles.

Publications Coordinator

1983 - 1986, Searway/McKenna/Morris/Planners, Raleigh, NC.

Wrote, edited, and submitted articles to professional/trade journal.

Associate Editor, The Biological Scientist

1980 - 1984, American Association of Biological Scientists, Tallahassee, FL.

Designed *The Biological Science Record*, a quarterly publication of the College of Biological Sciences.

Page 1

Professional Work Experience continued

Designer, Display Advertising Department

1976 - 1980, *Florida Sun-Times,* Tallahassee.

Designed advertisements, prepared layouts, created artwork and promotional ads, sold advertising; handled general administrative/recordkeeping duties; organized and conducted tours of the plant.

Relevant Activities

Member, Tallahassee Art Alliance, 1986 - present.
Volunteer, Children's Activity Center, 1991 - present.
Computer Graphic Art Workshop, Compaq Headquarters, Inc., Tallahassee, FL (one day).
Desktop Design and Publishing Seminar by Robert Parks, Tallahassee, FL (seven days).

References

Provided on request.

BRIAN WEBLEY 345 Coral View, Apt. 9B, Coral Gables, FL 33128, (305) 555-7823

OBJECTIVE

Production management position with a process-color printing firm

SUMMARY

More than 25 years experience in all aspects of printing technology and production
Technical background in publishing, graphic arts, printing, and systems
15 years in printing and department management
Developed innovative programs for cost-savings and increased productivity
Experienced mechanical engineer with thorough knowledge of printing equipment

CAREER EXPERIENCE

MANAGER OF GRAPHIC ARTS ENGINEERING   1988 to present
D.E.C. Printing Group, Southeastern Division, Miami, Florida
- Specified and managed $175 million in lithography for 12 printers in the division.
- Enhanced profitability as a result of involvement in procurement, planning, printing, and quality assurance programs, and the introduction of technological innovations.
- Directed 80 professional and technical people in 5 departments at the central plant.
- Worked closely with management in Quality Assurance/Target Management program, which increased efficiency by a margin of nearly 35 percent.

PRINTING OPERATIONS ENGINEER   1980 to 1988
Graphic Color, Subsidiary of D.E.C. Printing Group, Miami, Florida
- Operated and maintained working conditions for 7 Heidelberg 6-color presses.
- Designed work flow process that increased efficiency and press production by 20 percent.
- Supervised crew of 20 press operators and 5 technicians.
- Worked closely with stripping and camera departments to ensure highest quality press output.

TECHNICAL ENGINEER   1974 to 1980
Benberg-Lenz Manufacturing, Miami, Florida
- Worked as engineer on production development team.
- Assisted with design and testing of printing presses for color lithography.

EDUCATION

B.S., Mechanical Engineering, Arizona State University, 1974

ANGELINA BERGMAN

884 N.W. 12th Avenue
Fort Worth, Texas 76109
(214) 555-1985 (daytime)
(817) 555-9712 (evening and weekend)

SUMMARY OF QUALIFICATIONS

General management executive with 15 years experience in corporate sales, marketing, customer service, development, and distribution.

EXPERIENCE

DaMark-Dolin America Corp.   *1990 - current*

A $640 million Fortune 500 public corporation serving the cosmetics industry.

EXECUTIVE VICE PRESIDENT, Dallas, Texas
1994 - current

Catalog and Commercial Division. Direct sales, marketing, customer relations, and distribution for a two-plant, $180 million sales operation. Combined two acquired companies into the second-largest corporate division. Eliminated $325,000 in duplication costs. Designed national marketing strategy that produced a 15 percent sales increase. Generated 30 percent increase in new-business sales by expanding and upgrading product production. Increased profits by a margin of 23 percent in one year by enlarging client base and controlling prices. Improved quality control and productivity by reorganizing departments and centralizing support functions.

CORPORATE OFFICER AND VICE PRESIDENT, Houston, Texas
1990 - 1994

Corporate Management Division. Directed strategic acquisition business development, marketing, and venture subsidiaries. Directed major capital expenditures, business plans, and incentive programs for twelve business units. Formulated corporate mission and established long-range strategic plan, which led to supervision of major restructuring decisions. Completed several acquisitions and strategic divestitures that expanded the corporate profit margin approximately 18 percent.

Page 1

Angelina Bergman
Page 2

EXPERIENCE CONTINUED

DIRECTOR OF CORPORATE DEVELOPMENT, Houston, Texas
1983 - 1990

Corporate Management Division. Spearheaded four years of product design and diversification, resulting in the corporation's first major market breakthrough in the pharmaceutical industry. Managed all business and venture development, including acquisitions, new technologies, start-ups, joint ventures, and leasing agreements. Directed development of a new manufacturing line of medicinal lotions through acquisition of Soltero, Inc. Improved plant productivity by 15 percent.

EARLY CAREER POSITIONS   1975 - 1983

Operations Management, WemCo Inc., Houston, Texas
Design Module Leader, Patterson Corporation, Houston, Texas
Project Team Leader, Patterson Corporation, Shreveport, Louisiana

EDUCATION

Louisiana State University, M.S., Chemical Engineering & Business, 1983
University of Montana, B.S., Mechanical Engineering, 1975

REFERENCES AVAILABLE ON REQUEST.

KEVIN L. BAUER

3890 43rd Avenue
Ann Arbor, Michigan 48106
(313) 555-3892

CAREER SUMMARY

General management executive with significant broad-based experience in consumer, manufacturing, and publishing businesses. Technical background in publishing, graphic arts, printing, and systems. Proven leadership skills and expertise in:

Sales	Strategic Planning
Marketing	Business Development & Acquisitions
Operations Management	Financial Analysis

PROFESSIONAL EXPERIENCE

D.D. WILLIAMS CORPORATION, 1995 - Current

A $1 billion Fortune 500 public corporation serving niche printing and graphics/video markets.

Executive Vice President, Santo Catalog and Commercial Group, Ann Arbor, Michigan, 1997 - Current

- Directed sales, marketing, customer services, estimating, and distribution for a two-plant, $125 million sales printing operation.

- Combined two acquired companies into the second largest corporate business group, eliminating $250,000 in duplication.

- Designed a national, market-driven strategy which delivered a 17% increase in sales.

- Generated new business sales of 30% in response to expanded and upgraded manufacturing equipment requirements.

- Increased profits 28% through focus on prospecting and pricing control. Improved control and productivity by reorganizing sales assignments and centralizing sales support functions.

Corporate Officer and Vice President, Oshkosh, Wisconsin, 1993 - 1997

- Key member of Corporate Management (executive) Committee with broad strategic, acquisition, business development, and marketing responsibility and authority in lean and highly autonomous corporate structure.

- Directed major capital expenditures, business plans, and incentives for 12 autonomous business units. Key board member for venture subsidiaries.

Page 1 of 2

(PROFESSIONAL EXPERIENCE continued)

- Formulated corporate mission and market strategy which led to major restructuring decisions.
- Completed the purchase and transitionally directed the Peters Companies, adding five new subsidiaries and two new print markets and expanding sales by more than $200 million.
- Accomplished other acquisitions and strategic divestitures, including the sale of the Flexible Packaging Group (two plants, $50 million sales) and the decision to divest the video group (five companies, $45 million sales).
- Established the long-range strategy for the D.D. Williams Publications Groups (two plants, $43 million sales) and the strategic plan to create the D.D. Williams Pre-Press Group (three plants, $18 million sales), including the group management organization and start-up of Color Response-Minnesota.
- Spearheaded a corporate identity campaign which emphasized D.D. Williams's national scope; developed a new corporate name which sparked investor and Wall Street interest.

GREETING CARDS, Inc., 1975 - 1993

A $1.5 billion market leader in consumer and publishing products.

Director of Corporate Development, Kansas City, Missouri, 1989 - 1993

- Spearheaded four-year diversification program resulting in Greeting's first major acquisitions of Beel & Craig ($254 million sales) and SSN (educational, specialty, and consumer software publisher).
- Managed all business/venture development, including acquisitions, new technologies, start-ups, joint ventures, and licensing agreements.
- Directed an electronics venture and an acquired educational software subsidiary.

Manager of Graphic Arts Engineering, Kansas City, Missouri, 1985 - 1989

Operations Manager, Kansas City, Missouri, 1980 - 1985

EDUCATION

University of Massachusetts, Amherst, M.S., Industrial Engineering, 1979

University of Tennessee, Knoxville, B.S., Mechanical Engineering, 1977

JONATHAN B. OWENS
2245 RIVER ROAD
NEWPORT, OR 97366
(503) 555-2435

OBJECTIVE

After twenty years of active duty in the Coast Guard, I am seeking a management position in Program Development and Implementation that will utilize my extensive background in these areas.

EXPERIENCE

1995 - present: Branch Chief for Emergency Medical Central Training Center, U.S. Coast Guard, Newport, OR

Responsibilities
Developed, designed, and implemented the curriculum for training Coast Guard personnel. Responsible for selecting and evaluating staff of 30. Managed an annual budget of $200,000 for staff training and operations.

Contributions
Established new computer system to improve communications utilizing electronic mail. Developed and implemented new internal and external valuation programs to test new performance-based curricula. Designed and implemented new instructor development plans, which included continuing educational programs for personnel.

1993 - 1995: Operations Officer, U.S. Coast Guard, Ilwaco, WA

Responsibilities
Scheduled all ship movement activities. Supervised program for conducting boardings at sea to ensure compliance of commercial and recreational vessels to federal law. Supervised 20 personnel, including training and evaluation.

Contributions
Developed new unit training program by fostering a supportive educational environment.

1991 - 1993: Operations Officer, U.S. Coast Guard, Bethel, AK

Responsibilities
In charge of vessel traffic control for the safe passage of large crude oil carriers traveling in and out of Prince William Sound. Managed work schedules for both vessel traffic and communications watch standing personnel. Responsible for training, development, and performance evaluations for 15 personnel. Managed the maintenance of a remote microwave communications and vessel traffic radar system for all of Prince William Sound.

JONATHAN B. OWENS

Page 2 of 2

EXPERIENCE (cont.)

Contributions

Installed new radar tracking system which included upgrading remote power supply unit for one radar site. Improved personnel watch rotations to maximize time spent on the job as well as improve flexibility of time off. Implemented the hiring of civilian employees to replace Coast Guard personnel as permanent watch standers in the Vessel Traffic Center. Improved relations between Coast Guard and Maritime Industries.

1987 - 1991: Administration Officer, U.S. Coast Guard Marine Safety Office, Ilwaco, WA

Responsibilities

In charge of personnel and supply administration for a 50-person unit. Direct supervisor for seven personnel, including training and performance evaluations. Managed an annual budget of $350,000 for the maintenance and upkeep of an office building and a 29-unit housing complex.

Contributions

Centralized administrative personnel to take a team approach to handle all unit administrative matters. Eliminated unnecessary reports. Expedited the process of all administrative work by purchasing new computer hardware and software to increase efficiency.

1984 - 1987: Instructor, Leadership School, U.S. Coast Guard, San Diego, CA

Responsibilities

Involved with developing, designing, and implementing curriculum for newly established leadership and management program for Coast Guard personnel.

Contributions

Developed two-week curriculum for the school from the latest leadership and management practices. Participated in design, development, and testing of the new performance evaluation system currently used by the Coast Guard.

EDUCATION

Master of Arts in Educational Administration, University of Oregon, Eugene, OR
Bachelor of Science in Human Relations and Organizational Behavior, University of Oregon, Eugene, OR

REFERENCES AVAILABLE UPON REQUEST

Marcia Penas Smith

55 Alexandria Street, Apt. 25   Washington, D.C., 20013   (202) 555-0988

OBJECTIVE

A position as translator for a federal or state agency

LANGUAGES

Fluent in written and spoken Spanish, Portuguese, and French

EDUCATION

M.A. in Spanish and Portuguese, 1998, Middlebury College, Middlebury, VT
B.A. in French and Psychology, 1978, Arizona Sate University, Tempe, AZ
Foreign Study Program in Oaxaca, Mexico, 1975 - 1976

WORK EXPERIENCE

English Teacher, English Department, Madrid University, Spain, 1994 - 1996

Taught reading and conversation to undergraduates and teachers of non-English majors. Developed curriculum for and taught elective reading course on North American short stories. Taught beginning conversation to small group of primary school students. Informally advised Spanish students on living and studying in the U.S.

Assistant to Director, Office of International Education, Arizona State System of Higher Education, Arizona State University, 1986 - 1994

Developed and administered Latin American summer exchange program for high school students. Assisted with foreign student and foreign study orientation programs. Coordinated visits of international guests. Assisted in administration of foreign study programs.

Office Assistant, Office of International Programs and Summer Session, Arizona State University, 1978 - 1986

Assisted in administration of overseas programs. Assisted with information meetings and predeparture orientations. Gave general advising to students interested in study and work abroad. Handled summer session and special programs registrations. Responsible for general secretarial-receptionist duties.

ANNA ROBINSON
P.O. Box 389
Cheyenne, Wyoming 82001
(307) 555-2983

OBJECTIVE	To teach at the secondary school level
EDUCATION	M.Ed. and Certification, University of Colorado, Greeley, 1998
	B.A., Elementary Education, University of Michigan, Ann Arbor, 1987
	Wyoming Real Estate Broker's License, Rocky Mountain School of Real Estate, Cheyenne, WY, 1985
	Wyoming Real Estate Sales License, Professional Institute of Real Estate, Laramie, WY, 1981

RELEVANT EXPERIENCE

Reading and Writing Tutor and Student Teacher, Greeley School
District, Greeley, CO, 1997 - 1998

Advisor, Entrepreneurial Youth, Inc., Cheyenne, WY, 1986 - present
Classroom Teacher, Tyler School District, Tyler, MI, 1974 - 1981
Taught grades 1 through 7, specialized in Language Arts

PROFESSIONAL EXPERIENCE

Designated Broker, Sales and Marketing Director, Courtmore Homes, Inc.,
Cheyenne, WY, 1985 - 1996

- Responsibilities included development of purchase contract package; contract approval; design of brochures, advertising, model home complexes; consultation concerning land acquisition and development; hiring, supervision, and support of subdivision sales staff and decorating personnel.

Sales Representative, Homeland, Inc., Cheyenne, WY, 1981 - 1985

- Responsibilities included subdivision sales, contract writing, buyer relations and closings, and sales office/model complex management.

REFERENCES AVAILABLE ON REQUEST

PETER J. LUCERO

3876 Maple Street, Topeka, Kansas 66603

(913) 555-9835

CAREER OBJECTIVE

A career position in international relations or operations with a multinational corporation or major organization.

SUMMARY OF SKILLS

- Multilingual administrator, educator, lecturer in Spanish, German, French, and English.
- Associate pastor and director of a Chicago inner-city parish complex, an upwardly mobile Catholic community in Kansas, and a popular parish in Frankfurt, Germany.
- Regional consultant to the New York electronic media.
- Member, Board of Directors, for a nonprofit housing development corporation.
- Director of professional, paraprofessional, and volunteer staffs in four countries.
- Coordinator of private- and government-sponsored relief activities for Central American refugees.
- Chaplain and advisor to international business and diplomatic communities.
- Liaison between church authorities, civic officials, and professionals groups in the greater Frankfurt metropolitan area.
- Academic advisor to graduate students on University of Kansas campus.

CAREER HISTORY

Assistant Administrator, Associate Pastor, St. Mary's Church, Topeka, KS, 1997 - 1998

- As member of religious education staff, recruited, trained, and evaluated performance of 100 volunteer teaching/clerical support personnel.
- Created and conducted adult seminar groups, stressing contemporary moral and ethical problems.

Assistant Administrator, Catholic Archdiocese, Frankfurt, Germany, 1990 - 1997

- Initiated German-American lecture series on sociopolitical, moral, and religious themes.
- Regularly presided at multilingual liturgical functions in international congregations.
- Provided pastoral counseling, in three languages, to French, English, and German speaking communities in Frankfurt.
- Liaison between church officials and civic, business, and diplomatic leaders.
- Supervised educational programs for parish residents and their children.

CAREER HISTORY continued

Member, Administrative & Counseling Staff, Graduate Student, Jesuit College of Theology, Boston, MA, 1986 - 1990

- Served as academic advisor and pastoral counselor to resident graduate students while pursuing doctoral degree.
- Assisted in developing efficient administrative structures, challenging curricula, relevant practice, and appropriate criteria for the selection and training of those destined for ministry.

Assistant Administrator, Missionary Project, Tegucigalpa, Honduras, 1985 - 1986

- Served all levels of local, national, and international society in Honduras, from campesinos and refugees to professional and business classes and diplomatic personnel.
- Assisted in the pastoral and material care of these groups, focusing on the plight of displaced persons, the educational and health-care needs of indigenous populations, and the training and development of their civic, political, and religious leaders.
- Acted as liaison between these groups and international relief agencies.

Chaplain of St. Rose's Home, Chicago, IL, 1983 - 1985

- Served as chaplain at this home for terminally ill cancer patients.
- Attended to the spiritual, psychological, and counseling needs of patients and their families.
- Recruited, trained, and monitored performance of more than 100 volunteers.
- Performed traditional functions of active clergy in major urban hospital environment.

EDUCATION

St. Peter College, Newport, RI, B.A. Cum Laude, Sociology/Philosophy

Harvard Divinity School, Cambridge, MA, M.Div.

Jesuit College of Theology, Boston, MA, S.T.L. (advanced Master of Arts), Magna Cum Laude

Catholic Institute of Germany, Frankfurt, Germany, S.T.D./Ph.D. Candidate

REFERENCES AVAILABLE

JoAnna Weber

P.O. Box 34, Phoenix, AZ 85034
(602) 555-0938 or e-mail at weber@aol.com

Objective:

Office manager for travel agency, with opportunity to train in tour management.

Experience:

Office Manager, Saxton Microflox, Phoenix, Arizona
1997 - Present

Responsible for all central support operations, bookkeeping staff, and office planning and administration. Maintain payroll records, process federal and state tax reports. Handle cost accounting and general ledger reports. Direct hiring and supervision of office staff. Respond to requests from engineering and executive departments for special project support.

Travel Coordinator, Saxton Microflox, Phoenix, Arizona
1994 - 1997

Responsible for coordinating all travel arrangements for engineers and executives traveling nationally and internationally. Processed payments and payment vouchers. Maintained data file of travel resources.

Secretary, West Phoenix School District, Phoenix, Arizona
1985 - 1994

Provided secretarial support to principal and faculty. Extensive public relations contact with students, parents, faculty, and general public. Responsible for bookkeeping and supply inventory. Supervised central office staff.

Secretary, JKN Architects, Salt Lake City, Utah
1978 - 1985

Typed proposals and specification lists. Responsible for payroll and general bookkeeping. High level of public contact with contractors, clients, and general public.

Education:

A.A. Degree, Office Systems, Salt Lake Business College, Salt Lake City, Utah, 1978

References on Request

Joseph Monroe
3892 Beverly Road
Springfield, MA 01101
(413) 555-3982

Objective: A position in marketing and sales management at a radio station that would utilize my skills as a corporate executive and my extensive experience in sales management in the manufacturing field.

Education: M.B.A., University of Massachusetts, Amherst, 1990
B.A., Business Administration, Communications and Radio, Ohio University, Athens, 1974

Professional Experience:

As **Vice President of Sales & Marketing**, Amco Corporation, 1990 - present:

- Develop marketing strategies to support customer and operator needs.
- Coordinate between administrative, sales, and operations branches to provide manufacturing with standards and goals.
- Oversee relations with 50 top customers, representing more than $250 million in annual revenue.
- Supervise 20 sales staff and coordinate with Operations and Administration departments.
- Negotiated product and service charges with U.S. Postal Service, maintaining cost standard for a savings of $1 million over 5 years.
- Improved productivity by 45 percent in two-year period with design and implementation of employee participatory program.
- Supervised a marketing and promotion effort that saw sales improve 15 percent in the first quarter after implementation.

As **Sales and Marketing Manager**, Amco Corporation, 1975 - 1989:

- Supervised all sales people.
- Negotiated contracts with 20 top customers.
- Managed all customer fulfillment and complaints.
- Responsible for development and marketing of product changes and new services.
- Negotiated new and renewed contracts with 20 customers, representing an annual revenue of $100 million.
- Established a standard sales training program in-house, which improved efficiency and consistency in customer relations.

Page 1 of 2

(Professional Experience Continued)

As **Station Manager**, WIML Radio, Ohio University, 1973 - 1975:

- Managed budgets and staffing schedules.
- Supervised fundraising and programming, scheduling and publicity for radio station.

As **Programming Director**, WIML Radio, Ohio University, 1972 - 1973:

- Planned, reviewed, and revised all programming for station.
- Scheduled all on-air personnel.
- Hosted a classical and interview program.

Memberships:

Board member, Corporation for Public Radio, Massachusetts
Supporting member, Springfield Symphony
Member, Marketing Association of America

Professional and personal references furnished on request.

Juanita Rodriguez-Sutton
330 Hollywood Boulevard
Los Angeles, California 90063
(213) 555-2475 days
(213) 555-0248 evenings

Career Objective
Seeking position as Advertising Director for a large West Coast agency.

Achievements
- Handled distribution, retail marketing, advertising, and mail order marketing for weekly news magazine with more than two million circulation.
- Wrote advertising copy and made sales presentations to clients and account executives.
- Handled advertising accounts worth in excess of $1.5 million as Marketing Promotions Director for FM radio station.
- Obtained knowledge of domestic and overseas regulations for trademarks.
- Assisted marketing director with radio and television promotion and retail marketing.
- Coordinated radio and print interview opportunities for visiting artists and writers.
- Developed and implemented print and broadcast advertising campaign for major retail chain.
- Directed research department for market data and sales reports.

Work History
LA Productions Weekly, Los Angeles, CA
- Marketing Director, 9/98 to present
- Public Relations Director, 6/92 to 7/98

KBOQ Radio, Venice, CA
- Marketing and Promotions Director, 5/87 to 6/92
- Promotions Assistant, 3/87 to 5/87

Macy's, San Francisco, CA
- Marketing Department, 6/82 to 3/87

Education
University of California, Los Angeles
- Postbaccalaureate study in Advertising and Marketing, 9/90 to 6/92
- B.S. in Journalism/Public Relations, 6/82

JEAN K. SCHUMANN

389 SW 13th AVENUE   OLYMPIA, WA 97301   (206) 555-3982

CAREER OBJECTIVE

To obtain a position as Scientific Technician for the Washington Department of Fisheries or the U.S. Department of National Resources.

SUMMARY OF EXPERIENCE

- Collected biological data as Biological Aide at Washington Coastal Aquarium.

- Participated in field study emphasizing terrestrial vegetation, geological features, and marine organisms, and maintained field journal of activities, including plot studies.

- Participated in compiling environmental report for county sub-area plan, producing vegetation map, writing and editing sections of report, and presenting group results to planning committee.

- Maintained records of shipments, collected and prepared ore samples for chemical analysis, and assisted in surveying for Taber Shipments, Inc.

- Developed and implemented Marine Biology (Intertidal Organisms and Rocky and Cobbled Shore Habitat) and Cedar and Salmon Natural and Cultural History Programs for use at girl scout camps.

- Assisted in supervising and training staff, planning programs, and evaluating performance and programs.

- Taught and led nature activities for children and adults in marine and terrestrial biology, intertidal habitats and organisms, forest ecosystems and habitats, botany, zoology, and meteorology.

WORK HISTORY

Community Resources Staff, Campus Recreation Center, Deschutes University, Olympia, WA, 1995 - present

Assistant Director, Program Planner, Rainier Girl Scout Council, Tacoma, WA, 1990 - 1995

Program Development Intern, Rainier Girl Scout Council, Tacoma, WA, 1989

Biological Aide, Washington Coast Aquarium, Long Beach, WA, summers 1985 - 1989

Biological Assistant, Taber Shipments, Inc., Spokane, WA, 1984

EDUCATION

B.A. in Biology, Deschutes University, Olympia, WA, 1989

J. WILLIAM CLARK
4437 WHITE OAKS DRIVE
URBANA, IL 61801
(309) 555-2847 (VOICE)
(309) 555-3345 (FAX)

OBJECTIVE

An executive position in an organization involved with public policy and finance.

PROFESSIONAL EXPERIENCE

Lecturer, Management and Public Administration
Graduate Center, University of Illinois, Urbana-Champaign, 1989 to present

> Teach organizational management courses for the College of Business. Topics include Managing Organizations (process of organizing, planning, and controlling), Organizational Behavior (leadership, internal politics, and group dynamics), The Global Business Environment (domestic and international political, economic, and social issues that affect complex organizations), and Public Policy Administration (development, structure, and implementation of public policy).

Executive Consultant, Social Policy and Study Center
George Washington University, Washington, D.C., 1983 to 1989

> Developed and taught seminars on organizational management and global economic issues for officials from the governments of fourteen countries. Coordinated the development of an Equal Employment Opportunity Plan for a major public policy research organization. Represented senior management with the government auditing agency requiring the affirmative action plan. Other principal clients included the Economic Policy Research Institute, the American Center for the Study of Behavior, and W.W. Group International, an organization that monitors and analyzes public policy issues throughout the world.

Assistant Executive Director, National School Boards Association
Washington, D.C., and Chicago, Illinois, 1978 to 1983

> Planned, organized, developed, and coordinated programs and activities for the national network of school district trustees from the nation's urban centers. Consulted with the Director of the President's Commission on School Finance, the Executive Director of the Education Commission of the States, and the National Advisory Committee on Career Education.

page 1 of 2

PROFESSIONAL EXPERIENCE *(continued)*

Program Associate, National Public Schools Support Association
Washington, D.C., 1975 to 1978
> Held full financial accountability for budgeting, planning, controlling, and personnel management. Provided consulting services to school districts and support organizations nationally.

Previous employment includes three years as a public school teacher in Illinois and four years active duty as an officer in the U.S. Navy.

EDUCATION

Ph.D. Politics and Public Policy Administration
George Washington University, 1982

M.B.A. Finance and Administration
Purdue University, 1975

B.A. Business and Economics (NROTC)
Purdue University, 1970

MEMBERSHIPS

National Field Task Force for the Improvement and Reform of American Education, U.S. Office of Education

Retired Naval Reserve Officers Association

REFERENCES ON REQUEST

KARL LI

290 Summit Drive
Portland, Oregon 97208
(503) 555-0709

OBJECTIVE: A management position in sales or promotion for a quality manufacturing corporation.

PROFESSIONAL EXPERIENCE:

Executive Director (April 1996 - present), Willamette Valley Health Care Foundation, Portland, Oregon

> Provide direction for the Foundation. Responsibilities include strategic planning, fundraising, program development, volunteer development, and grant writing. Produce, sponsor, and coordinate the annual festival, Healthfest. Conduct a needs assessment for Willamette Valley as a measure of program effectiveness. Plan annual community fundraising campaign and membership campaign. Serve as Vice President of Oregon Non-Profits Association. On Portland Regional Hospital Finance Committee; Willamette Community Health Council, Oregon.

Regional Director (1991 - April 1996), The Children's Foundation, Chicago, Illinois

> Provided strategic management and hands-on assistance to 11 chapters in 9 states. Offered expertise in fundraising, finance, volunteer development, staff training, and programs. With chapter directors, established goals and objective for chapter performance. Evaluated achievements against goals. Hired, trained, and supervised chapter directors and regional offices staff. Directed 115 employees. Planned and conducted two training meetings per year for chapter directors and other key staff/volunteers. Acted as a resource to other regional directors on the subject of budgets, finance, and quantitative analysis. Served on the board of The National Children's Foundation, 1993 - 1996. Established a volunteer, region-wide database consisting of executive committee members and key volunteer leadership in 1993, with annual updates.

Page 1 of 2

PROFESSIONAL EXPERIENCE continued:

Executive Director (1989 - 1991), The Children's Foundation, Midwest Region, Des Moines, Iowa

> Responsible for the administration of the local chapter, including fundraising and program development. The door-to-door campaign led the nation in per capita revenue, the highest per capita to date, anywhere in the nation. Our largest sponsor-based event, Lifewalk, was expanded to the point where every community of 5,000+ held the event. Improved collection procedures and enhanced revenue. Influenced a reversal of Des Moines School Board policy to allow The Children's Foundation access to schools for fundraising.

Special Events Consultant (1988 - 1989), Des Moines, Iowa

> Created two major fundraising events: bike treks and backpacking treks. Developed volunteer and corporate resources for special event fundraising in an agency heavily dependent on mail income.

Karl Li Advertising and Public Relations (1987 - 1988), Des Moines, Iowa

> Provided advertising and public relations services to a variety of clients, both profit and nonprofit. Specialized in radio production/advertising.

Account Executive (1985 - 1987), KUMO Radio, Chicago, Illinois

> Serviced and sold accounts. Wrote copy and assisted in production. Director for Mutual Radio, Midwest. Provided live feed and delayed commercials for Central time slots.

EDUCATION:

Master of Public Administration (MPA), University of Chicago, 1987
Bachelor of Arts, Communications (BA), University of Chicago, 1985

REFERENCES AVAILABLE ON REQUEST

LUCINDA ALVAREZ
1283 Bramble Drive
Austin, TX 78710
(512) 555-1701 home ~ (512) 555-3602 office

OBJECTIVE   To obtain a position as senior technical editor for a large corporation

EDUCATION   Columbia University, M.A., English. GPA, 3.91. 1997

Columbia University, B.A. with Distinction, Phi Beta Kappa, English with Creative Writing Emphasis. 1980

Additional coursework included chemistry, calculus, geology, statistics, and computer science.

EXPERIENCE

1995 - present   **Proposal Writer,** Corporate & Foundation Relations, University of Texas Office of Development, Austin, TX

Assist administrators and faculty in writing and editing a broad range of grant proposals for technical and lay audiences. Develop, write, and design public relations and fundraising materials for the university's maximum priority projects. Review annual reports and other corporate publications to identify major donor prospects. Conduct quarterly seminars for staff and faculty on proposal writing. Supervise student assistant. During first year was involved in generating gifts to the university totaling more than $3.1 million.

1998 - present   **Board of Directors, Fundraising Chair,** Wild Rose Press, Austin, TX

Hold volunteer administrative and fundraising responsibilities for small nonprofit literary press. Write and edit grant proposals to government agencies and private foundations.

1990 - present   **Freelance Writer, Graphic Designer, and Photographer,** Austin, TX

Services include color and black-and-white photography, desktop publishing, and writing and editing newsletters, catalogs, advertisements, feature articles, and public relations materials. Recent project involved researching and writing science biographies for technical reference book.

Page 1 of 2

EXPERIENCE (cont.)

1985 - 1995   **Promotions Assistant,** University Book Stores, Inc., Austin, TX

Responsible for writing, designing, and producing store brochures, flyers, signs, and advertisements. Required extensive knowledge of desktop publishing, graphics, and production methods.

1980 - 1984   **Program Manager and Events Coordinator,** Drake's Books and Magazines, New York, NY

Responsible for public relations and all aspects of weekly reading series at NYC's third largest independent bookseller. Designed and wrote all advertising copy, press releases, catalogs, brochures, and employee training manuals. Scheduled author appearances and hosted and introduced authors at events with audiences ranging from 50 to 400. Authors included Pulitzer Prize-winners Taylor Branch and Tracy Kidder and National Book Award-winner Stephen Jay Gould. Supervised a staff of two.

REFERENCES   Current references and writing samples available on request.

TAMARA MESERVEY

389 Southwest Fifteenth Avenue
Philadelphia, PA 19104
(215) 555 - 2899

GOAL: A production management position in advertising on a large circulation newspaper.

QUALIFICATIONS:

- Experienced in all aspects of printing and prepress processing equipment.
- Marketing, advertising, sales, and graphic production.
- Records management, including accounts payable/receivable, payroll, inventory control, and tax reporting.
- Purchase of supplies to assure adequate inventories.
- Day-to-day management responsibilities, including scheduling, assigning activities, training, and program assessments.
- Experienced with computerized typesetting and prepress graphic production.
- Public relations skills, including reception, sales, collections, and purchasing.
- Time management proficiency, promoting timely completion of projects and meeting deadlines.

EDUCATION:

Community College of Philadelphia, Pennsylvania, 1997 - present

Business management courses with emphasis in retailing, advertising, marketing, accounting, and human relations.

Philadelphia College of Art, Pennsylvania, 1981 - 1983

Associate of Arts Degree, Process and Camera Stripping.

EXPERIENCE:

Management Assistant, Regional School of Ballet, Philadelphia, 1991 - 1998

Duties: Learned and implemented managerial skills in daily management of dance school. Arranged advertising through local media sources. Planned development and marketing and advertising strategies. Completed billing reports, payroll records, compiled accounts payable and receivable information. Collected unpaid balances. Ordered and maintained inventories. Supervised staff and scheduled work hours.

Page 1 of 2

EXPERIENCE CONTINUED:

Camera Operator/Printer, Sir Speedy Printing, Philadelphia, 1988 - 1991

Duties: Operated variety of camera and bindery equipment, including printer and plate maker. Assisted customers, completed sales transactions and reports, prepared advertising for local media and yellow pages. Began system of tracking advertising results to better determine advertising cost-effectiveness.

Printer, In and Out Printing; Philadelphia, 1983 - 1988

Duties: Operated printing machine and darkroom equipment. Coordinated incoming work assignments. Performed paste-up, platemaking, and bindery duties. Trained newly assigned employees. Composed, printed, and generated monthly newsletter.

REFERENCES AVAILABLE

Theresa Miller

33528 Santa Monica Boulevard, Los Angeles, CA 90088 (213) 555-8842

Career Objective

Traffic manager for an advertising agency or corporate advertising department.

Work Experience

Connections Magazine, Hollywood, California

Production Manager, 1998 - present

Oversee all aspects of production and printing for a national publication. Involved in extensive client and advertising agency contact. Organize all art, mechanicals, and final films. Coordinate with editorial and advertising department heads for positioning of advertising. Work with graphic designers on production specifications and proofing. Handle in-depth contact with other media and service vendors. Produce copy and mechanicals for advertisements.

L.A. Arts Weekly, Los Angeles, California

Advertising Manager, 1990 - 1998

Directed advertising sales for 45-page arts section of *L.A. Times*. Developed sales strategies, assigned territories to sales staff, conducted weekly sales report meetings, tracked sales and billing. Coordinated advertising design and production with graphic design staff. Directed preparation of mock-up ads for sales presentations to encourage regular, increased ad sales for target clients. Developed special ad pages for arts organizations and directed sales efforts.

Havener's, Burbank, California

Assistant to Promotions Director, 1984 - 1990

Conducted all in-store promotions and coordinated special events for large department store. Placed advertising and publicity notices in local media. Wrote text for radio and television spot announcements. Consulted on grand opening of Hollywood store. Provided customer assistance.

Page 1 of 2

Education

University of California, Los Angeles

B.S. in Advertising and Marketing, 1984

Honors:

Cum Laude, 1984

Dean's List, 1982 - 1984

Wilma Morrison Scholarship, 1981 - 1984

National Association of Student Yearbooks, Advertising Sales Award, 1984

Best Advertising Design, 1984

Memberships

American Advertising Association

Women in Advertising

American Marketing Association

Magazine Publishers Inc.

References provided on request

ALETHA BESSEY
4893 ARLINGTON AVENUE
INDIANAPOLIS, INDIANA 46201
(317) 555-9889
bessey@aol. com

OBJECTIVE
A position in marketing with a strongly customer-oriented, multinational corporation.

PROFESSIONAL EXPERIENCE

Research Scientist, International Feminine Care, Beverly Jones Corporation, Indianapolis,
1997 - present

- Evaluate, recommend, and develop product changes to meet performance expectation of a new feminine care product for three international regions of this Fortune 500 multinational, consumer products company manufacturing such brand products as Bouncies and Comforts.
- Establish quantitative measures for subjective functional performance evaluations and product comparisons.
- Work closely with international marketing research department in suggesting and implementing improvements to consumer market research questionnaires.
- Design product development plans for market research efforts.
- Obtain medical clearances, coordinate materials, prepare product samples, and schedule equipment and testing.
- Work with U.S. product development group to integrate United States and international program support.
- Provide engineering with product information for equipment designs.
- Participate in regional project update meetings in the United States, Asia, Latin America, and Europe.
- Provide support to process trials in Mexico and Taiwan.
- Prepare reports on product functional tests.
- Participate on Product Development Seminar Committee to define format for company-wide seminar.

Scientist II, Scientist I, Senior Research Technician, Beverly Jones Corporation,
Indianapolis, 1987 - 1997

- Accountable for all aspects of product development for industrial wipers and washroom towels.
- Successfully developed new washroom hand towel product that out-performed market leader and returned twice the initial sales projections.

Page 1 of 2

(PROFESSIONAL EXPERIENCE cont.)

Scientist II, Scientist I, Senior Research Technician, Beverly Jones Corporation Indianapolis, IN (Cont.)

- Developed new market research techniques to define consumer language in describing products; translated and interpreted terminology for quantitative measures.

- Developed and validated mathematical model for determining user preference from physical test data.

- Developed several line extension products and implemented cost-saving technologies for existing products.

- Member of multifunctional business team; assisted in defining market needs, designing products to meet cost requirements, verifying advertising claims, providing technical sales support, and implementing product roll-outs.

- Managed project budgets and established project objectives.

- Analyzed and resolved customer complaints regarding product performance; conducted one-on-one customer interviews and site visits.

- Provided process and product support for start-up of a new converting mill.

- Advised manufacturing personnel in conversion operations to ensure product quality and specifications; assisted in trouble-shooting efforts.

- Wrote product specifications for manufacturing guidelines and worked with Quality Assurance for test methods and quality procedures.

- Consulted with packaging specialists to define packaging specifications.

Quality Assurance Superintendent, Techmill, Inc., Youngstown, OH, 1981 - 1987

- Organized and managed fifteen-person quality department for a new nonwoven cloth manufacturing plant.

- Implemented corporate quality programs.

- Trained personnel and implemented statistical process control systems throughout the plant.

- Wrote and implemented a GMP manual for Class III medical device.

EDUCATION

M.B.A., Kennesaw State College, Kennesaw, GA, 1981
B.S., Mathematics/Engineering, University of Minnesota, Crookston, MN, 1979

REFERENCES AVAILABLE UPON REQUEST

GAVIN McCLOUD   P.O. Box 12, St. Paul, MN 53402 (612) 555-0932

OBJECTIVE

A position as a high school science teacher

EDUCATION

University of Minnesota, Twin Cities, Minneapolis, MN, 1998, Master of Education

University of Vermont, Burlington, VT, 1972, Bachelor of Science

PROFESSIONAL CERTIFICATION

Minnesota: Elementary 1 - 6

Middle and High School, 7 - 12

RELATED SKILLS AND EXPERIENCE

Taught classes in stream ecology, outdoor survival, backpacking, and trip planning. Supervised overnight trips for primary and secondary school students. Assisted in programs and designing courses aimed at integrating science education with outdoor activities.

Assisted in research on stream ecology and effects of pollutants: collected samples and other data, performed literature searches, and compiled and condensed information.

Prepared data summaries, chart illustrations, and graphs; wrote summary reports; evaluated methods, procedures, and results of stream ecology studies.

Assisted in biological studies to assess natural and artificial habitats by woodland species for developing habitat protection, mitigation, and enhancement criteria.

EMPLOYMENT HISTORY

Instructor, Minnesota Outdoor Center, St. Paul, MN
Part-time staff, 1994 - present

Biological Assistant, State of Minnesota Wildlife Department, Minneapolis, MN
1972 - 1994

References provided upon request

PAULA R. ROPER

38402 Butte Lane
Fargo, North Dakota 58502
(702) 555-2908

PROFESSIONAL OBJECTIVE

A position as Customer Service Representative in a retail or service environment.

SKILLS HIGHLIGHTS

- Skilled at assisting clients, customers, and the public.
- Work well independently and as a member of a team.
- Work with thoroughness and attention to detail.
- High quality work in WordPerfect 6.1 and Lotus 1-2-3.

EMPLOYMENT HISTORY

Administrative Assistant, City of Fargo, Fargo Fire Department, 1996 - present
Perform receptionist duties, answering inquiries and complaints. High volume of word processing and data entry of budget documents. Data entry and recordkeeping of Fire Incidents and Training Records. Process purchase orders. Team member of FireMed ambulance subscription program.

Municipal Court Clerk, City of Fargo, 1987 - 1996
Completed recordkeeping for court. Initiated court correspondence, prepared court docket. Compiled statistical reports. Prepared and submitted court budget.

Administrative Assistant, Nuclear Engineering Department, North Dakota State University, Fargo, 1983 - 1987
Interacted with public, student body, and potential clients of research teams as main receptionist for department. Maintained undergraduate student records. Compiled statistical reports. Completed typing of technical manuscripts, scientific reports, and correspondence.

EDUCATION

University of Oregon, Eugene, Oregon, 1983, B.A. in Liberal Arts and Letters
Mt. Angel College, Mt. Angel, Oregon, 1979 - 1981, Liberal Arts Major

References Provided Upon Request

SUZANNA M. RENAULT
389 King Court
Springfield, MA 01101
(413) 555-2938

OBJECTIVE

An associate-level position in a public relations firm.

EXPERIENCE

Production Director, Cable Newscenter 7
Cable News Network, Springfield, MA, 1990 - present
Supervise the development and airing of a one-hour cable news show. Edit video footage. Handle all video while on air. Develop and maintain strong communication with director, creating consistency in the show's format. Provide support in maintaining the flow of material.

Operations Engineer, WHHH-TV
Massachusetts Broadcasting Company, Springfield, MA, 1985 - 1990
Provided technical support and assistance for morning and mid-morning news and commercial breaks, both local and network.

Public Relations Assistant, TIC AM/FM Cable
Springfield College, Springfield, MA, 1984 - 1985
Supervised the public image presented by radio station. Organized a Charity Bowl-a-Thon, which raised $2,000 for the Children's Care Center of Springfield. Produced and co-wrote an audio documentary about radio for local high school students. Developed and distributed press releases for all station activities. Acted as mediator during internal conflict.

EDUCATION

Bachelor of Arts, Speech Communication, University of Massachusetts, Amherst, 1984

Hannah Tober Scholarship for student showing greatest potential in the field of Communications Management, 1984

REFERENCES AVAILABLE ON REQUEST

DONNA SAWYER   3890 Park Avenue, Chicago, IL 60607   (312) 555-2998

OBJECTIVE

A position in a federal or state agency involving administration and project management

SKILLS HIGHLIGHTS

<u>Management</u>:
Program and project management, staff supervision, budget preparation and administration, public relations, staff development, human resources recruitment and selection, union contract interpretation and administration, Affirmative Action and EEO compliance planning and administration.

<u>Communication</u>:
Team building, employee relations counseling, dispute resolution and mediation, public speaking, report writing, group facilitation.

<u>Financial</u>:
Financial analysis, cash flow analysis, securities analysis, business and economic forecasting, project feasibility analysis, market analysis.

<u>Computer</u>:
Prime Mainframe, IBM, Macintosh, Lotus 1-2-3, Excel, Statview, 1-2-3 Forecast, WordPerfect, and MS Word.

PROFESSIONAL EXPERIENCE

<u>Consultant</u>, Hoffman & Monroe, Inc., Chicago, IL, 1990 - present
Providing business consulting services which include market analysis, marketing planning, strategic planning, public relations, and budgeting. Projects: Market research and business planning; human resources consulting regarding EEO and Affirmative Action guidelines, hiring strategies and practices; statistical analysis; and project planning and administration.

<u>Partner</u>, Sawyer, Collins & Co., Inc., Chicago, IL, 1980 - 1990
Principal in firm providing marketing analysis and planning, business forecasting and planning, and financial analysis for private firms and corporations.

EDUCATION

B.A., Business Administration and Management, University of Chicago, 1980

REFERENCES AVAILABLE ON REQUEST

Daniela A. Jamas

71 S.W. 15th Street, Sacramento, California 95814 (916) 555-7321

Objective

A staff management position in a human resources firm or in a corporate human resources department.

Related Experience and Skills

- Developed and provided one-day seminars and a ten-week adult education class in social services advocacy through Pacific Community College.
- Experienced with group participation, lecture, and one-on-one instructional techniques.
- Supervised a staff of ten to develop community-wide needs assessment; set training goals and objectives; developed an audience-appropriate curriculum; coordinated speaker schedule; evaluated training results.
- Tutored middle-school students with special needs on a one-on-one basis.
- Coordinated social services to help individuals meet their needs for support, counseling, resources, and information in other support services.
- Worked closely with government, private social service agencies, and businesses to integrate services that best met individual needs.
- Implemented, produced, and edited various newsletters; wrote articles for several magazines.
- Familiar with IBM computers, well versed in Macintosh word processing and database programs.
- Semifluent with both written and spoken Spanish.

Work History

- *Office Manager,* Environmental Consultants, Inc., Sacramento, CA, 1995 - present
- *Marketing Director,* All Seasons Windows, Sacramento, CA, 1991 - 1995
- *Telemarketing Director,* Raymond Bros., Inc., San Jose, CA, 1989 - 1991
- *Manager,* The Book Cover, San Jose, CA, 1986 - 1989
- *Manager,* Information and Referral Department of Public Affairs, Sacramento, CA, 1982 - 1986
- *Teacher's Aide,* Highland View Middle School, San Jose, CA, 1981 - 1982

Education

San Jose State University, B.S., 1981
Recreation and Leisure Studies, with minor in English

References available upon request

ANNA GUPTA
3892 Barbary Road
Sacramento, CA 95813
(916) 555-9283

OBJECTIVE

Buyer/Manager for an independent bookstore

EDUCATION

1980 M.L.S.　　University of Washington, Seattle
1975 B.A.　　　Comparative Literature, University of California, Berkeley

PROFESSIONAL EXPERIENCE

1990 - present　*Director, Media Services*
West Sacramento School District

Direct the library services of 20 elementary, middle, and high schools in district. Supervise ten professionals. Designed the high school library media center of 50,000 print and nonprint items.

1985 - 1989　*Head Librarian*
Berryman School Library, Sacramento, California

Directed the acquisitions and functioning of this school library serving 1,200 students and 95 professionals. Supervised five para-professionals.

1980 - 1985　*Acquisitions Librarian*
Timberland Regional Library, Olympia, Washington

Served as acquisitions librarian for this regional branch of libraries.

1975 - 1980　*Teacher, Literature and Writing*
St. Mary's Girls Academy, Olympia, Washington

Taught literature and writing courses to high school students at this private high school.

REFERENCES AVAILABLE ON REQUEST

Alfred D. Landers
728 Bolero Court
Novato, CA 94945
(415) 555-2943

Objective

To play an integral role on a pastoral care team in a hospital or mental health facility.

Education

Training Center for Spiritual Directors, Taos Benedictine Abbey, New Mexico, 1998. Intensive initiation into the art of spiritual direction.

Healing Ministries, Institute of Ministries, San Jose, CA, 1995 - 1997. Formation and Advanced training, four semesters.

Clinical Pastoral Education, Mental Health, Western Coast Hospital, San Jose, CA, 1994 - 1996. Internship, four units.

Pastoral Experience

1997 - 1998   Community Member, Taos Benedictine Abbey
Participated in counseling and prayer ministry with retreatants; participated in liturgies, retreats, and business office activities. Will complete training with an additional month-long program next year.

1994 - 1997   Chaplain intern, Western Coast Hospital
Pastoral focus on mentally ill legal offenders. Provided Eucharist ministry to patients in medical, surgical, neurological, geriatric, and adult psychiatric units. Participated in liturgy and prayer services. Provided pastoral interviews and counseling, including many religious denominations and nondenominational.

Page 1 of 2

Job History

1984 - present   Senior Commercial Lines Underwriter, Umbrella Insurance, Group Department, San Rafael, CA
Handle Oil Jobbers program in commercial group department, a nation-wide program with heavy casualty, property, and inland marine coverage. Responsible for six states totaling in excess of $6 million annual premiums. Implemented company changes in underwriting practices and procedures. Developed 10-step program for profit. Audited current files.

1980 - 1988   Personal Lines Underwriting Supervisor, Umbrella Insurance, San Rafael, CA

1975 - 1980   Property and Casualty Underwriter, Umbrella Insurance, Newark, NJ

References upon request

Maria Nelson
226 Highline #299
Albuquerque, NM 87102
(505) 555-3872

Objective

A management position in television or radio advertising in which my marketing and management experience can make a strong contribution to the organization as a whole.

Work Experience

Seven-Eleven, Albuquerque, NM

Regional Marketing Director, 1995 - present

Developed a successful marketing campaign for a convenience store chain. Implemented marketing strategies to increase sales by 23 percent at the least profitable outlets. Initiated and maintained a positive working relationship with radio and print media representatives. Designed a training program for store managers and staff.

Arizona Register, Phoenix, AZ

Advertising Sales, 1990 - 1995

Sold space advertising to a variety of business and organizational clients. Maintained excellent communications with top clients. Made cold calls on businesses to encourage advertising. Responsible for 25 percent increase in regular advertiser base over four-year period. Coordinated with design and production departments to maintain quality in advertising products as client advocate.

Arizona Evening Herald, Phoenix, AZ

Classified Advertising Sales; 1986 - 1990

Sold classified advertising to private and business clients. Entered advertisements in computer system. Checked advertisements for accuracy. Billed clients for advertising. Made follow-up calls to increase run of advertising. Coordinated with advertising department on special issue discount offers in the classified section.

Other work experience includes advertising sales manager for student radio station, University of Arizona; sales clerk for women's clothing boutique; and door-to-door sales representative for children's books.

page 1 of 2

Education

University of Arizona, Phoenix, AZ

Bachelor of Science in Business, 1986. Major: Advertising and Marketing.

Minor: Communications.

Honors: Project Award for advertising campaign developed for student radio station

Dean's Honor Roll

Sigma Delta Gamma, advertising honorary

Seminars

Marketing Strategies in Advertising, American Marketing Association, 1998

Cooperative Advertising: Opportunities and Strategies, Arizona Press Association, 1995

References available on request

ROBERT L. WILSON JR.

1854 S. Franklin Ave., Chicago, IL 60647 (312) 555-8376

Objective   A position with a literary arts center or arts advocacy agency.

Experience

10/94 -
Present

Week's Worth Magazine, Chicago, IL

Editor and Designer. Started weekly arts, culture, and entertainment magazine, gaining a circulation base of 14,000 within four months. Manage all aspects of marketing and promotion. Supervise advertising department staff for ad sales and self-promotion advertising campaigns. Manage all aspects of production. Assign staff articles and edit freelance articles for publication. Design magazine from cover to cover. Manage budget and payroll for 15-person staff.

4/92 - 9/94   *Friday's Magazine*, Illinois Daily News, Normal, IL

Editor. Assigned and edited staff stories. Created page layout and design. Wrote feature-length stories. Managed budget and 8-person staff for weekly entertainment magazine supplement to college newspaper.

8/89 - 4/92   College of Arts & Sciences, Illinois State University, Normal, IL

Feature Writer and Columnist. Covered various entertainment events, wrote feature stories and weekly commentary column for Features department.

1/84 - 8/89   Communications Department, Illinois State University, Normal, IL

Staff Writer. Community Relations Department. Assisted in the writing, design, and layout of a 12- to 24-page alumni newsletter.

Education

B.A. Communications (Fine Arts Minor), Illinois State University, Normal, IL, 1984

Honors

Critical Film Review Award, Second Place, Illinois College Press Association

Graphic Illustration Award, Second Place, Illinois College Press Association

Public Relations Society of America

GEORGETTE ANDERSON
389 Spring Rock Road
Missoula, MT 59806
(406) 555-2009

OBJECTIVE

- A position in Human Resources Management for a manufacturing corporation.

QUALIFICATIONS

- Design systems for recruiting, selecting, and training clerical, production, and middle management personnel.

- Maintain and direct recruitment, selection, and training of those personnel.

- Develop, monitor, and implement EEO/AA policy and Affirmative Action Plan.

- Investigate and process complaints relating to EEO/AA.

- Develop corporate policy manual of EEO/AA.

- Conduct EEO/AA seminars and presentations.

WORK HISTORY

Publicity Manager, Rocky Mountain Products, Missoula, MT, 1993 - Present.

> Hired as first Communications Manager of this wood products company to develop and implement a public relations effort.

Assistant Personnel Manager, Rocky Mountain Products, Missoula, MT, 1988 - 1993.

> Assisted in recruitment, selection, and training of clerical, production, and management personnel.

Assistant Manager, Corporate EEO Programs, U.S. West Communications, Richmond, VA, 1980 - 1988.

> Shared responsibility with corporate EEO/AA Officer for monitoring equal employment opportunity and affirmative action activities for 95 corporate locations nationwide.

EDUCATION

> B.A. in Communications, 1977, Mary Baldwin College, Virginia

Amelia Nelson
1545 Arboretum Drive, Apt. 34
Rutland, Vermont 05701
(802) 555-3828

OBJECTIVE   A corporate position in sales that involves extensive customer contact.

WORK
EXPERIENCE   *Public Relations Assistant*
Applebury Inc., Burlington, Vermont, 1995 - present.
- Direct interface with clients and the public, assessing needs and providing solutions. Assist in product inquiries and setting up discounting programs for qualified customers. Represent company in trade shows. Exhibit strong product knowledge in handling customer complaints through analysis and evaluation of complaint report. Support for sales force and on-site technicians.

Management/Marketing Assistant
Divan Management, Rutland, Vermont, 1985 - 1995.
- Assisted marketing research projects and conducted a general management survey for mini-warehouse industry. Coordinated promotional campaigns, utilizing database analysis to focus on target market.

Special Promotion Assistant, Sideline Sales
University Bookstore, Burlington, Vermont, 1982 - 1985.
- Responsible for selecting, ordering, and promoting the sales of sportswear to organizations and a student body of 40,000 students, averaging more than $75,000 in sales. Demonstrated skill in leadership, organization, and group motivation.

Entrepreneur
Nelson Promotions, Burlington, Vermont, 1980 - 1982.
- Sold custom-made sportswear to Greek system and dormitories. Examined and evaluated on- and off-campus markets through on-site observations and informal interviews. Supervised two employees.

EDUCATION   B.A., 1980, Business and Marketing
University of Vermont, Burlington

REFERENCES AVAILABLE ON REQUEST

Peter L. Larson 3890 Peach Road, Atlanta, GA 30304   (404) 555-9888

Objective   A position in the manufacturing industry that will utilize my extensive background in sales and sales management.

Summary of Qualifications

Results-oriented sales professional recognized for ability to develop and maintain productive long-term relationships with clients.

Excellent track record of establishing new sales territories and attracting new clients.

Expert in developing effective long-range marketing plans.

Strong training and motivational skills, as demonstrated by the success achieved in developing successful sales teams.

Outstanding public speaker with the proven ability to conduct effective and persuasive seminars and presentations.

Successful at projecting accurate sales and budget forecasts.

Experience

1990 - present   U.S. Flyers, Chatham County Airport, Georgia
Assistant Director/Ground School Manager
Developed student enrollment for career flight academy. Utilize direct mail, telemarketing, and direct sales approaches to cultivate and qualify prospective students. Develop relationships with beneficial markets. Present promotional talks and seminars at job fairs, college campuses, and civic organizations. Act as liaison between students and school administrators. Monitor students' programs to ensure completion within designated time and budget parameters.

1987 - 1990   Workshops, INC., Atlanta, Georgia
Sales Director
Developed direct mail, sales plans, and marketing/advertising promotions for training workshops. Created and implemented sales training programs. Analyzed sales promotion efforts and developed new strategies. Expanded client base, securing several key corporate accounts. Increased business by 20 percent during the first year.

Page 1 of 2

(Experience continued)

1983 - 1987   Sales Corporation of Tallahassee, Florida
               Sales Trainer
               Organized and presented sales training seminars.

1978 - 1983   U.S. Navy, Miami, Florida
               Midshipman
               Served on Commanding and Executive Officers staff.
               Awarded Sailor of the Month and Quarter.

Education

Bachelor of Business Administration, NROTC, 1978
Memphis State University, Memphis, Tennessee
Dale Carnegie Institute, 1985 - 1986
Awarded: Achievement, Human Relations Award; Special Award for Achievement;
   and Highest Award for Achievement

Activities

- Chair, Membership and Marketing Committee, Atlanta Country Club, 1994 - 1995
- Member, City Country Club, 1990 - 1995
- Fundraising Team, Atlanta Performing Arts, 1992 - 1995

References Available on Request

Susan L. Jeffers // 2235 S.W. Hammond // Laramie, Wyoming 82057 // (307) 555-9872

Career Goal

Communications Director in a corporate environment

Demonstrated Skills

Experienced with marketing and public relations: developing marketing strategies and campaigns, dealing with sensitive issues with the news media, and developing and projecting an organization's most positive image.

Ability to develop plans, goals, strategies, and timelines, and to maintain schedules and analyze results of projects.

Ability to work independently and exercise sound judgment.

Excellent communications skills, both in writing and in making public presentations to small and large groups on a variety of topics.

Ability to work effectively with the public, elected officials, board and committee members, program operators, and staff in a teamwork environment.

Experienced in grant-writing and fundraising.

Thorough knowledge of state and federal government operations and regulations affecting business in the state.

Experienced with preparation and production of graphics materials, including brochures, newsletters, and annual reports.

Knowledge of newspaper advertising department practices in advertising sales, placement, and design.

Professional Experience

Research Specialist, Public Relations Department, State of Wyoming, June 1994 to present

Professional Experience (cont.)

Advertising Sales, Laramie Evening News, Laramie, Wyoming
January 1992 to May 1994

Advertising Production, Sheridan Sun, Sheridan, Wyoming
August 1988 to November 1991

Advertising Intern, Laramie Evening News, Laramie, Wyoming
June to August 1988

Education

B.A. in Journalism/Advertising, University of Wyoming, Laramie,
1988

Won AASA award for design of print advertising campaign

References are available upon request

ARTHUR LEWIS

789 HARBOROUGH STREET
BOSTON, MASSACHUSETTS 02169
(617) 555-8962

objective   to find employment in a human services field which offers new challenges and opportunities and utilizes the experience, skills, and knowledge from nearly 20 years of increasing responsibility in the education field.

specific strengths

creativity   ability to synthesize diverse ideas into coherent concepts, to think in new directions, and to assist others in more clearly stating their ideas and objectives

tolerance   ability to work with a diverse population and enjoy the interaction and challenges of diversity; essentially team-oriented and a "people" person

assessment   ability to employ various standard and non-standard assessment processes as well as mature insight in the evaluation of programs and proposals

writing   ability to write informally and formally, imaginatively as well as in a scholarly, more research-directed style

speaking   ability to present challenging concepts in formal oral presentations; strong small group skills and experience; significant teaching ability with diverse student population

education

M.A.   Education, 1983, University of Massachusetts, Boston, MA

B.A.   African American Studies and American Literature, 1980, Boston University, Boston, MA

employment history

Language Arts Department Head, Jamaica Plain High School, Jamaica Plain, MA. 1998 - present. Coordinate curriculum planning and implementation. Act as department liaison to school board and administration. Teach English, Creative Writing, Technical and Research Writing, American Literature, British Literature, and Multicultural Literature. Supervise the production and publication of a student literary magazine.

Page 1 of 2

employment history continued

English and Writing Instructor, Jamaica Plain High School, Jamaica Plain, MA.
1990 - 1998. Taught English, Creative Writing, Technical and Research Writing, American Literature, British Literature, Multicultural Literature, and Speech to high school students. Tutored remedial and advanced students of Literature and Writing. Served as faculty sponsor of African American Student Union.

Language Arts Instructor, Franklin Junior High School, West Roxbury, MA.
1985 - 1990. Taught English, Reading, Speech, and Writing classes to 7th and 8th grade students. Faculty sponsor and advisor for the Student Drama Group.

Substitute Teacher, South Boston Districts, Boston, MA.
1983 - 1985. Taught Language Arts classes in junior and senior high schools in South Boston.

references available on request

Maryanne Barbaras
38549 Palm Lane, Hialeah, Florida 33010
(305) 555-3088

OBJECTIVE

To utilize proven skills in planning and managing programs and employees to help children's advocacy organization and manage its services.

EXPERIENCE

Manager, Customer Support, Peyton Products, Inc., Hialeah, Florida, 1996 - present

MAJOR ACCOMPLISHMENTS:

- Reorganized and combined the Manufacturing Order Service Department and Sales Customer Service Department into customer-sensitive customer support group.

- Developed procedures, systems, and a team concept to better utilize skills and talents while increasing productivity.

- Designed WORK program to promote a "quality of service" approach to customer relations.

- Coordinated the conversion of a new order system as well as participated in the formal design of the integrated sales/manufacturing system.

- Developed various inventory programs and systems to increase responsiveness to customer product requirements.

- Implemented programs designed to increase staff motivation to achieve positive growth through goal setting and recognition.

- Managed a staff of twenty professionals and nonprofessionals.

Manager, Order Service, Peyton Products, Inc., Hialeah, Florida, 1985 - 1995

MAJOR ACCOMPLISHMENTS:

- Reorganized the three domestic and international order service product groups into one organization.

- Developed unifying procedures and a cooperative working environment.

- Developed closer interdepartmental alignment, improving production scheduling to meet customer product requirements.

- Developed closer interdepartmental alignment with the customer service group to improve order/production status for improved customer relations.

- Increased staff development activity through conference attendance, advanced degree encouragement, and product group team leadership.

page 1 of 2

EXPERIENCE (cont.)

Customer Service Representative, Peyton Products, Inc, Hialeah, Florida, 1982 - 1985
Teacher, Lincoln Middle School, Tampa, Florida, 1976 - 1980

EDUCATION

Columbia University Graduate School, September 1982
Two-Week Seminar/Certification, Market Analysis for Competitive Advantage

Florida State University, 1976
Bachelor of Arts, History

REFERENCES AVAILABLE UPON REQUEST

JEAN HANAKA

3829 Deering Street, Apt. 23A, Portland, ME 04101   (207) 555-2483

Objective:

A position as staff photographer for a public relations firm or university communications department.

Education:

B.F.A., Photography, New England Institute of Art, Maine, 1998

Coursework in Art and Photography, South Central Community College, Buffalo, New York, 1976 - 1977

B.S., Liberal Studies, Plainfield College, Plainfield, Vermont, 1975

Professional Experience:

1987 - present, *Office Coordinator*, Community Relations Office, University of Southern Maine, Portland, Maine

Produce educational and promotional material (copy and photos) for many campus events and displays, both on and off campus. Write advertising copy for both radio and newspapers. Design and assist in designing advertising layout for newspapers. Establish and reorganize procedures for maintaining records, billings, and follow-up; organize detailed record keeping for the Speaker's Service; initiate surveys and tabulation of area rental rooms, prices, and contract persons. Write office guidelines, including an office procedures manual. Maintain campus maps, staff directory, and new employee packets. Monitor and assign work to four classified staff and supervise three to six work-study students.

1984 - 1987, *Senior Secretary*, Community Relations Office, University of Southern Maine, Portland, Maine

Assisted the Community Relations Director. Maintained office records. Coordinated room reservations, Speakers' Service functions, and assignments for the Graphics area of the CRO.

1976 - 1984, *Staff Photographer*, Learning Resource Center, Buffalo, New York

Provided photographs for LRC Newsletter, biannual bulletin, and promotion and publicity use. Researched community events, local news, and trends for news and photography leads. Attended all LRC events. Completed layouts of newsletter and bulletin.

Portfolio and references available upon request

RAOUL HARMON
910 NE 223rd #937, Brooklyn, NY 11201   (718) 555-2909

Objective

A position in the promotions department of a publishing house

Work Experience

Customer Service Assistant, 1997 - present, Academic Book Service, Inc., Brooklyn, NY

- Research problems with library book shipments using custom C-Basic database, searching both archived records and current orders with publishers.
- Prepare documentation for library book returns for credit, and reorder correct books when required.
- Contact publishers for price and availability information regarding library orders.
- Determine type of credit issued, securing evidence involving discrepancies with library orders and actual books received.

Book Purchasing Clerk and Sales and Promotion Assistant, 1990 - 1997,
Blue Water Gallery and Shop, New York, NY

- Responsible for book ordering and stocking.
- Assisted with merchandising.
- Assisted with production of publicity materials (fliers, signs, posters, invitations).
- Responsible for customer service and sales.

Senior Editor, 1982 - 1990, Blackman East, Inc., Newark, NJ

- Proofread and compared academic and public libraries' Series Authority file records against Library of Congress Authority file to standardize catalogued records.
- Edited records and bibliographic files using Basic language on an IBM terminal.
- Researched problem heading and series updates.

Education

B.A. 1981, City College of New York, NY

Philosophy and Literature

References available upon request

Sandra B. Walters
334 Northwest Vineland Ave., Concord, NH 03321 (603) 555-2214

Career Interest: Outward Bound Instructor in Mountain Climbing Division

Important Skills & Experience:

- First American woman to climb Tengeboche Himal in Nepal.
- Completed solo 1,000 mile trek in Chilean Andes.
- Made ascent to 21,000-foot elevation on Everest before weather ended expedition.
- Climbed seven major peaks in the Cascade Mountain Range in Oregon and Washington.
- Organized and led climbs to four major peaks in Rocky Mountains in Colorado and Wyoming.
- Organized and led treks on the Pacific Crest Trail from Canada to Mexico.
- Wrote book (as yet unpublished) on experience trekking in Third World countries.

Related Work Experience:

- Taught high school history in public schools for 12 years.
- Provided counseling assistance in program for drug-dependent youth.
- Taught short courses in backpacking and mountain climbing for local sporting goods store.
- Taught courses and led trips for university student outdoor recreation center.

Employment History:

History Teacher, South Concord High School, 1990 to 1998
History Teacher, Washington Lee High School, Boston, 1986 to 1990

Additional Work Experience:

Real Estate Sales, Central Home Realty, Boston, 1980 to 1986
Secretary, Central Home Realty, Boston, 1976 to 1980

Education:

Coursework in Counseling, University of New Hampshire, 1996 to 1998
B.A., History, Boston University, 1986

References available on request

WANDA ELAINE FARBER
14 East First Street, Wichita, KS 67231
(316) 555-6129

GOAL:

Develop a challenging career in sales leading to management in marketing and sales.

PREVIOUS EXPERIENCE:

Office Manager, Martin Accounting, Inc., Wichita, Kansas, 1998 - present
Handle all bookkeeping and office staff personnel responsibilities. Maintain payroll and ledger sheets. Monitor employee productivity and activity reports. Review actuarial expenditures and income periodically in accordance with budgeted figures. Work with owner to develop planning and financial reports.

Gift Shop Sales Clerk, St. Joseph's Hospital, Wichita, Kansas, 1992 - 1997
Responsible for stocking inventory, making and recording sales, balancing daily receipts, and closing gift shop after hours. Provided assistance to hospital visitors seeking gifts and greeting cards for patients. Responded to queries from nursing staff and doctors. Delivered floral bouquets as required.

Cashier, Wal-Mart, Wichita, Kansas, 1988 - 1992
Trained new employees on cashier's responsibilities and procedures. Made sales, recorded transactions, and balanced cash drawer at end of shift. Assisted with restocking. Answered questions for store patrons.

Childcare Provider, Little Ones Day Care Center (Self-Employed), Marquette, Iowa, 1978 - 1988
Started private day care center with two employees caring for fourteen children, ages eighteen months to five years. Developed and implemented preschool curriculum for older children. Provided informational newsletter to parents of children in the center.

Page 1 of 2

EDUCATION:

Continuing Education, Falls City, Community College, Wichita, Kansas
Completed fourteen credit hours in Marketing through the Business Department; currently enrolled in Management Systems and Finance.

Associate Degree, Business, Central Community College, Cedar Rapids, lowa
Coursework focused on business management, finance, and accounting.

REFERENCES:

Available on request

Stephan Monett
34 South Avon Street
Charleston, South Carolina 29411
(603) 555-2236

Career Objective

Senior Manager leading to Project Director position

Career Achievements

• Direct, supervise, and administer turnkey projects from inception to start-up for equipment manufacturing firm.

• Coordinate with sales department to review system process design, equipment, sizes, schedule, and engineering costs before presenting final proposal to the client.

• Negotiate purchases and advise corporate president and CEO of pending contracts and negotiations.

• Completed 17 domestic projects and 20 international projects in Latin America, South America, Spain, and Africa.

• Conceived, initiated, and successfully sold design of two new equipment products that resulted in a 40 percent increase in corporate sales over two years.

• Completed all projects on or ahead of schedule. All projects resulted in corporate profits; many produced higher profits than anticipated.

• Instituted procedures for project documentation handling and project communication.

• Trained project engineers and project managers to design and manage assigned projects.

• Instituted program for college interns and developed training program that culminated in job offers to those graduates whose performance met challenges of the position. After seven years, all students thus hired are still with the company and highly productive.

• Supervised four project management teams, including 12 engineers and 16 drafters.

• Acted as site project engineer during construction of $250 million plant.

• Registered professional engineer in the states of South Carolina and Arkansas.

Page 1 of 2

Career Experience

Senior Project Manager, DRG Inc., Charleston, South Carolina, 1988 - present
Senior Project and Process Engineer, Hopewell Systems, Charleston, 1984 - 1988
Process and Plant Engineer, Toverston Dryers, Little Rock, 1981 - 1982
Pilot Plant and Process Development Engineer, James River Corporation, Neenah,
    Wisconsin, 1977 - 1981

Education

M.S., Chemical Engineering, Georgia Institute of Technology, Atlanta, 1988
B.S., Engineering, University of Wisconsin, Milwaukee, 1977

Professional References Available as Requested

Chapter 6

Sample Cover Letters

15 March 20__

Human Resources Director
Search Committee: Senior Technical Editor
Merrick Engineering, Inc.
P.O. Box 223
Rutland, Vermont 05702

To the members of the Search Committee:

Enclosed is my application for the technical writer/editor position currently available at Merrick's Rutland office.

From the Environmental Computing Center to the new University Theatre and an endowed professorship in integrated circuit design, I have written, edited, and coordinated more than 150 grant proposals for many of the University of Vermont's most significant projects. As proposal writer for the University Foundation and Development Office, I work closely with vice presidents, deans, directors, and faculty to present their projects to both lay and technical audiences. I directly supervise two staff members and a student assistant, and coordinate the efforts of others involved in grant writing and fundraising processes within the University.

My graduate work in English and undergraduate studies in pre-medicine at Stanford have prepared me to write with ease on a variety of topics. I've edited complicated research presentations for many of the university's premier scientists while also working with leading scholars in the humanities to prepare fundraising documents for various cultural programs.

My experience as a freelance writer, graphic designer, and photographer further qualifies me for this position. Two of my recent publications present biographies and in-depth research abstracts on scientists featured in *Nobel Prize Winners: Physiology and Medicine*.

Your prospectus requested salary requirements. As my primary interest in the position is in the challenges it offers to put my skills to good use for a company that has a strong international reputation for excellence, I would be satisfied should the proposed remuneration meet my current gross annual income of $45,000, which includes salary and benefits.

I will be out of town until the 19th, after which I will be happy to meet with you. I would value the opportunity to join the strong and growing team at Merrick, and I appreciate your review of my application.

Sincerely,

Amada Wentworth
26 West Parade Drive
Rutland, Vermont 05702
(802) 555-9847

J. WILLIAM CLARK
4437 WHITE OAKS DRIVE
URBANA, IL 61801
(309) 555-2847

May 11, 20__

Mr. Arthur Davidson
Director
Davidson & Beckfield Associates
Suite 110, Ridley Tower
Chicago, IL 60621

Dear Mr. Davidson:

I was delighted to talk with you yesterday about your interest in hiring a public affairs director, and I want to restate my interest in learning more about the position.

So that you might learn more about my background, I have enclosed a summary resume for your review. If you prefer, I can forward my complete dossier, along with recommendations from professional associates.

What captures my interest about this position is the possibility for effecting change on a significant scale. My previous experiences have offered tremendous opportunity for influencing the country's growth in positive ways, but within fairly limited spheres: education and domestic economics, primarily. I have continued my involvement with social policy and public administration while lecturing at the university, and I am more convinced than ever that there is a great need for an organization like yours to turn its attention to unifying these issues in a direct and meaningful way. That is a challenge I would find immensely rewarding, both personally and professionally.

Our mutual friend, Helen Ashwood, told me I could find no more professional and respected an organization with which to align my efforts. After the discussion you and I shared this morning, I clearly agree with her astute assessment.

Therefore, I look forward to talking with you again soon.

Best regards,

Bill Clark

February 21, 20___

Frank Martin
Jones Construction Co.
3356 Highway 36
Pocatello, Idaho 83251

Dear Mr. Martin:

I am writing to apply for the foreman's position listed in the Human Services Division Office. My resume is enclosed. It lists my previous work experience.

For the past 15 years I have worked as the supervisor at Twin Peaks Plywood Mill, where I was responsible for 24 workers on a shift. I also scheduled workers for two other shifts. The closure of the mill has prompted my return to construction work, which I did successfully as a union carpenter for nearly 10 years.

I believe my construction background together with my supervisory experience provide the qualifications you are looking for in a construction foreman. I have worked on both single- and multiple-family housing as well as several-story office buildings and am familiar with building codes in Idaho as a result of building my own home.

I would like to call and make an appointment to talk with you, or you can reach me at 555-6682. Thank you for considering my application.

Sincerely,

Joseph W. Caldwell
346 Buena Vista
Pocatello, Idaho 83251
(208) 555-6682
(E-mail) aol@buildit.com

Angelina Bergman
884 N.W. 12th Avenue
Fort Worth, Texas 76109
(214) 555-1895 (daytime)
(817) 555-9712 (evening and weekend)

21 March 20__

Corrine Bracken
Executive Director
Design Engineering
20 West Tenth
Dallas, Texas 76443

Dear Ms. Bracken:

In reply to your advertisement in the *Wall Street Journal*, March 15, I am enclosing a professional resume and letters of recommendation for the position of vice president of sales and marketing.

I believe the executive management positions I've held with DaMark-Dolin American have given me the experience and capabilities you are looking for in a top marketing executive. As DaMark-Dolin has recently been acquired by InnaVail Corp., I have chosen to seek new opportunities and challenges within the corporate management sphere.

I have taken the liberty of calling to arrange for an appointment to speak with you further in order that I might learn more about your expectations and how I might make a significant contribution toward Design Engineering's future progress and growth. I look forward to meeting with you on April 5.

Best regards,

Angelina Bergman

Darius G. W. Harms
3485 Plainfield Road
Lincoln, Nebraska 68573
(402) 555-9287

March 1, 20__

Jonathan Parker
Engineering Division Director
State of Nebraska
P.O. Box 5678
Lincoln, Nebraska 68570

Dear Mr. Parker:

Please accept this letter and the enclosed resume in application for the Engineering Supervisor position announced February 25.

I believe my extensive background in structural and mechanical engineering meets or exceeds the qualifications you are looking for. I have served both as a senior engineer and as an engineering supervisor with responsibility for 120 workers.

For my part, I would like to put my expertise and experience to work for the benefit of public works projects, where safety and quality form the guiding values, as stated in your position description. Too often in the corporate world, the demand for higher profit margins takes precedence over innovative developments and worker safety. My experience in this field, however, has given me the ability to achieve desired results in the most efficient manner possible, thus cutting costs and increasing productivity.

Please review the enclosed resume and call me at the number above. I would like very much to talk with you about the position and what my experience can bring to your department.

Sincerely,

Darius Harms

Margaret Samuelson
3131 Mountain Drive
Longmont, CO 80501
(303) 555-2435

April 1, 20__

Susan Franklin
Personnel Director
Specialist Books
P.O. Box 2362
Denver, CO 80235

Dear Ms. Franklin:

Please accept the enclosed resume and letters of recommendation in application for the Senior Editor position with the Science & Technical Division of Specialist Books. I am responding to the position announcement listed in the March 26 edition of *Publishers Weekly*.

Currently I am managing editor of the University of Colorado Press, with full responsibility for acquisitions, development, design, and production. The position has been an extremely rewarding one, but statewide budget cuts within higher education have resulted in indefinite closure of the press.

Therefore, I would like to put my energy and extensive publishing background to work for Specialist Books in your Science and Technical Division. Approximately 65 percent of the titles I published with the UC Press were of a scientific or technical nature, and I gained additional editorial experience in the field as Editorial Assistant of the Environmental Studies Department of the university.

I would be happy to forward copies of relevant publications, both initial manuscripts and final publications, as examples of my editorial work. I would also appreciate an opportunity to discuss the position with you personally. I can be reached at the above number after hours and on weekends, and at 555-0429, ext. 23, during the week.

I look forward to receiving your call and thank you in advance for your consideration.

Yours sincerely,

Margaret Samuelson

GLORIA SANTOS 2534 Collins Avenue, Miami, FL 33239 (315) 555-8906

March 25, 20__

Pat Newton
Personnel Director
Lane Michaels Associates
345 Main Street
Miami, Florida 33219

Dear Pat Newton:

In response to the March 18 advertisement for a Financial Resources Associate in the *Miami Herald*, I am submitting the enclosed resume and salary requirements for your consideration.

For the past 13 years, I have worked as an accountant and office manager for a variety of organizations. My interest in the financial resource management of these organizations led me to return to graduate school at the Florida International University for a certificate in financial management, which qualifies me as a financial resources counselor and securities adviser.

My coursework involved extensive study of economic theory, policy, and practice, as well as the specific methodologies of financial analysis and resource management. My previous experience as an accountant served me well in pursuing study in these areas, and I believe it has allowed me to bring a unique perspective to the analysis and management of finance.

I would like to meet with you to discuss the position and your requirements in more detail as well as present further support for my specific qualifications for the position. I am available at the number above any day after 2:00 p.m., and on weekends. I look forward to talking with you, and thank you for your consideration.

Sincerely,

Gloria Santos

1233 Mission Street
San Pablo, California 98329

January 20, 20__

Personnel Director
Bakersfield & Associates
Box 123
San Pablo, California 98332

Dear Director:

Please accept the enclosed resume in application for the position of associate sales director, which was advertised in the *San Francisco Chronicle* last week.

After an interesting and rewarding career as an engineer, I returned to graduate school to pursue a growing interest in business, specifically in marketing and sales. Early in my career, I gained some valuable experience as the Engineering Sales Specialist for Shell Oil Company. In this position, I worked with manufacturers and small business owners to coordinate efforts for fuel efficiency and cost savings. The marketing and sales program that resulted was the most successful sales program in the company's history.

During my graduate program at Oregon State University, I worked closely with several faculty members in consultation with a major technology manufacturer in the area to recast the company's image and stimulate sales in a slow economy. The strategic planning sessions with corporate executives provided a tremendous on-the-job training opportunity for me as a graduate student, and the project achieved the desired results.

My inquiries have revealed that your firm has a strong reputation for excellence and innovation that makes me eager to bring my skills in strategic planning and market analysis to work for Bakersfield & Associates.

I would appreciate an opportunity to discuss the position with you further. Please call me at (212) 555-0812, where messages may be left if I am personally unavailable.

Thank you for your consideration.

Sincerely,

Donna Everson

Joan P. Yolen

20876 Hopewell Ave., Aurora, IL 60571 (847) 555-3833

February 19, 20__

Andrew Martin
Executive Director
Sheraton Hotel
600 Shoreline Drive
Chicago, IL 60615

Dear Mr. Martin:

I am enclosing my resume and three letters of recommendation in reply to the position announcement for Personnel Director at the Chicago Sheraton Hotel.

I believe you will find that my experience has provided me with the qualifications you are looking for in your top personnel officer. I have held several managerial positions with responsibility for personnel issues, including handling union negotiations and safety regulations. I am also well versed in payroll accounting and the required quarterly tax reports.

As you will note from the enclosed letter from my current employer, David Harris of Jordan Distributing, the downsizing of the corporate management structure has left no clear path for advancement within the organization. While I have enjoyed my tenure with Jordan, I am interested in taking on new challenges, particularly in the area of personnel management.

Once you have reviewed the enclosed material, I would appreciate an opportunity to talk with you further. I can be reached at 847-555-3833. I look forward to talking with you.

Thank you for your consideration.

Sincerely,

Joan P. Yolen

143 MW 19th
Everett, WA 98215

March 13, 20___

Mr. Jack Dunn
Superintendent
Everett School District
P.O. Box 16394
Everett, WA 98235

Dear Superintendent Dunn:

John Nukes in your department recommended that I write to you to express my interest in the Associate Principal's position currently being advertised for the Everett Junior High School. Enclosed you will find a summary resume.

After several years with increasingly responsible positions in the Bethel School District in Alaska, I have returned to my home town with the desire to continue my career in education administration. I believe my educational background and classroom and special programs experience give me the qualities needed to be a successful associate principal.

Most recently I was involved in a special project to develop an incentive program for boosting school attendance. The program brought together a broad base of community support and provided an opportunity for children to learn more about their own cultural backgrounds as well as that of others in the community. It was a tremendous success. At a time when educational support from taxpayers is faltering, it is imperative to develop timely, location-specific programs to get people reinvolved in our schools. I look forward to the challenge of stimulating my home town to greater public support for the school programs.

I will call your office early next week to schedule an appointment to speak with you further about the position and my qualifications. If you would like to reach me before then, I am available at (206) 555-9283. I look forward to meeting with you soon.

Sincerely,

Andrew Vizenor

Robert L. Wilson Jr.
1854 S. Franklin Ave.
Chicago, IL 60647
(312) 555-8376

January 19, 20__

Jane K. Shapiro
Director of Development
Art Exhibitors of Chicago
16 Bayshore Drive
Chicago, IL 60602

Dear Ms. Shapiro:

I am very interested in applying for the position of Communications Specialist in the Development Department. Enclosed are a brief summary and some samples of publications for which I have served as editor and designer.

As a member of the cultural "scene" in Chicago for the past ten years, I have lately felt a need to get more directly involved in helping the arts continue to thrive, not just survive. Toward this end, I have recently begun looking for positions in which I could take an active role in arts support and advocacy. I believe my dedication as well as my skills in the communications media will serve the position profitably.

After you've had an opportunity to review the enclosed material, I would like to meet with you personally. I can be reached at the above number, or I will call you by the end of next week to schedule an appointment. I am eager to talk with you further about the position and how I envision my contribution to your organization. Thank you for your consideration.

Sincerely,

Robert L. Wilson Jr.

MAIA JOINER   24 Wellington Place, Tallahassee, FL 32311 (904) 555-6787

January 16, 20__

Susan Winslow, Director
Public & Corporate Relations Department
Hammond Powell Hyde and Carter
24 W. Broadway, Ste. 1215
Tallahassee, Florida 32301

Dear Ms. Winslow:

Please accept this letter and the enclosed resume in application for the position of public relations associate for broadcast production currently open at Hammond Powell Hyde and Carter.

For the past 25 years, I have worked in the broadcast media industry and gained a wealth of knowledge of media affairs, public interests, and corporate communications. I believe the perspective I bring from my background on the "other side of the fence" will serve me well in your department.

My technical background in electronics and video technology have also proven invaluable when producing video programs and advertisements. With a thorough understanding of how such a program is made, I can use the medium to its best advantage.

I would like to show you some footage from several of the projects I have worked on, both recently as production engineer for the Channel 5 News at Noon and from my tenure as public relations associate for WJKE-FM Radio.

Thank you for your consideration. I look forward to hearing from you.

Sincerely yours,

Maia Joiner

Arthur Lewis
789 Hanaborough Street
Boston, Massachusetts 02169
(617) 555-8962

February 21, 20__

Dr. Frank Parminter
Executive Director
Department of Health and Human Services
452 Center Street, Suite 3305
Boston, MA 02135

Dear Dr. Parminter:

Thank you for sending the information I requested concerning the Public Information Officer position currently available with your department. I would like to apply for the position, and am enclosing my resume and the requested letters of recommendation and salary requirements.

I can bring to this position some unique skills gained through several years as a language arts instructor in the high school system. Teaching writing and communication skills is perhaps the best possible way to expand and refine one's own skills as well as knowledge of production processes for printed publications.

I would like to have an opportunity to talk with you further about the position and the specific strengths I can bring to your department. I will call your office early next week to schedule an appointment at your convenience.

I look forward to meeting you and learning more about the program areas the department covers. Thank you for your kind attention.

Sincerely,

Arthur Lewis

Juanita Rodriguez-Sutton
330 Hollywood Boulevard
Los Angeles, California 90063
(213) 555-2475 days
(213) 555-0248 evenings

March 26, 20__
Jefferson Grant
Director
Hollywood Ad-Man
443 La Ciernica Boulevard
Hollywood, California 90028

Dear Jeff:

I enjoyed talking with you Thursday about the A.D. position with Hollywood Ad-Man. After our discussion, I came away convinced that I'm the woman for the job. Once you've reviewed the enclosed resume and agency list, I believe you'll agree.

You mentioned that one area not currently covered by staff members' experience is research and market analysis; you've had to contract this work out or rely on hunches and suppositions. I can bring extensive experience in both areas to take some of the guesswork out of strategic planning and target advertising.

I've also had significant experience with broadcast media, both radio and television. Given the trend in advertising today toward a reliance on cable television outlets, additional experience in this area could be a strong plus for your company.

I will call you next week to talk more about the job and what I can bring to the position. Again, I enjoyed our conversation and look forward to meeting with you soon.

Best regards,

Juanita Rodriguez-Sutton

Tucker Wendell
P.O. Box 12597
Cincinnati, Ohio 45204
(513) 555-9041

March 18, 20__

Glynnis Martin
House of Imoja
1257 S. Patterson
Cincinnati, Ohio 45212

Dear Ms. Martin:

I am writing in application for the youth training coordinator's position announced in Sunday's issue of the *Cincinnati Gazette*. Enclosed please find a resume and statement of philosophy, as requested in the position description.

Your program works with disadvantaged youths of various ethnic backgrounds, and I believe I am highly qualified for the position, not because I have all kinds of degrees in psychology or sociology, because I don't. My qualifications lie in my having been right where these kids are when I was their age, faced with the seemingly insurmountable odds against any kind of success. I learned the hard way to set my sights on achievable goals, then go after them one step at a time, always believing in my ability to succeed. Perhaps more than anything these young people need role models who have shared their feelings of discouragement but who have carved their own new directions and new meanings of success.

As employment and training manager for Food-Pac Corporation, I have worked extensively with young people, many of them high school dropouts, who saw a job on the food processing line as the dead end of their dreams. By developing a program of cross-training, which allows workers to train in areas of special interest in addition to the line work, I have been able to help many youths see a new pathway and go on to achieve a different dream.

I found this the most rewarding aspect of my job, and as a result have become involved in a variety of youth-oriented programs. I would now like to devote my attention full-time to helping stem the crisis among our youth, especially those living in urban areas like Cincinnati. I hope to talk with you soon to discuss your program and how I can contribute to its success.

Please call me after 5 p.m. or on weekends at the number above, or I can be reached during the day at 555-2785, ext. 213. Thank you for your consideration. I look forward to hearing from you.

Sincerely,

Tucker Wendell

KARL LI
290 Summit Drive
Portland, Oregon 97208
(503) 555-0709

April 16, 20__

Sibyl Jameson
Vice President, Marketing & Sales
Simmons & Wooster, Ltd.
21 Grand Street
Portland, OR 97210

Dear Ms. Jameson:

I was delighted to talk with you yesterday about the sales manager's position currently open at Simmons & Wooster. As you requested, I am forwarding a summary resume outlining my previous experience in the world of nonprofit corporation development. I have also enclosed some sample publications produced under my direction at both the Willamette Valley Health Care Foundation in Portland and the Children's Foundation in Chicago.

In many ways, the worlds of fundraising and sales are very closely related. In both, one asks a potential patron to part with hard-earned income in exchange for some kind of return. With fundraising, my job was to persuade patrons of the value of such intangible returns as a lasting kindness or a tax deduction come April 15th. Marketing also plays an extremely important role in fundraising activities: presenting a strong "corporate image," the need to keep the corporation in the public eye, and "selling" a potential donor on something as elusive as a concept.

In my familiarity with the quality of the products and service provided by Simmons & Wooster, I can say with certainty that developing and directing sales campaigns will be both stimulating and rewarding. I am looking forward to our April 26 meeting so that we can further discuss your expectations for this position and how my background will allow me to bring some fresh insights to the role of sales manager.

With best regards,

Karl Li

FAITH NGUYEN   775 S.W. Tillbury Road, Fresno, CA 93723   (203) 555-7623

February 6, 20__

Ms. Ellen Carlson
Senior Director
California Department of Economic Development
One Government Plaza
Sacramento, California 95813

Dear Ms. Carlson:

Thank you for the information you sent in regard to the Project Manager's position with the CDED. I would like to submit the enclosed application and resume for your further consideration.

I have worked with the Consortium of California Counties for several years, and I believe I have found my niche in the area of project management. I have handled a wide range of projects with increasing levels of managerial responsibility. Most recently, I directed the planning, coordination, and management of a major statewide conference on job training, which involved the participation of several international specialists. I was given less than two months to arrange the entire project, and yet the results received appreciative reviews from all participants.

After a long and rewarding tenure with the Consortium, however, I am aware that I have reached the extent of opportunities for advancement within the organization. Therefore, I am looking forward to new challenges, and would very much like to join the impressive program at CDED.

I can be reached at (209) 555-2984 during the days, and at the number above for messages as well as evenings and weekends. I look forward to hearing from you and discussing how I might contribute to your program.

Sincerely,

Faith Nguyen

BRIAN WEBLEY
345 Coral View, Apt. 9B, Coral Gables, FL 33128 (305) 555-7823

February 27, 20__

Personnel Director
Patterson Printing
Box 1263
Miami, Florida 33551

Dear Sir or Madam:

I am writing to apply for the Production Manager position advertised in Sunday's edition of the *Miami News*. Enclosed is my resume and statement of salary requirements.

In my 23 years with the printing industry, I have worked primarily as a mechanical or operational engineer concerned with the technical end of printing machinery. More recently, I have developed an interest in and discovered a facility for managing the front end of the business: production and press preparation. As manager of Graphic Arts Engineering and the D.E.C. Printing Group, I took on increasing responsibility for the management and facilitation of the production processes in addition to the engineering concerns of the equipment. During my tenure in this position, I implemented programs that increased efficiency by approximately 35 percent and thus significantly increased the company's profit margins.

By concentrating my energies more fully on production management, I believe I can achieve significant gains for Patterson Printing as well. Once you have reviewed the enclosed material, I would like to talk to you further about your organization and how I might become a part of your team.

I look forward to hearing from you.

Sincerely,

Brian Webley

JONATHAN B. OWENS
2245 River Road
Newport, OR 97366
(503) 555-2435

31 March 20__

J. Paul Murky
Executive Director
Human Resources Consortium
State Office Complex, Suite 743 B
Salem, Oregon 97310

Dear Mr. Murky:

After twenty years of active duty in the U.S. Coast Guard, I am ready to move inland and take on new challenges in a civilian career in program development and implementation. I would like to bring my experience in training and curriculum development to work for you in the position of Management Specialist III. In response to the position announcement, I am submitting the enclosed application for your review.

My most recent responsibilities with the Coast Guard involved the development, design, and implementation of a curriculum for training Coast Guard personnel in emergency response and medical training. I was responsible for selecting and evaluating a staff of 35 for the Central Training Center. In addition, I established a new computer system to improve communications, which utilized electronic mail and enabled instant communications with Coast Guard facilities around the world.

I would like to speak with you personally about the position and my unique qualifications. Please call me at the number above, and I will be delighted to travel to Salem to meet with you at your convenience.

Thank you for your consideration. I look forward to talking with you.

Sincerely,

Jonathan B. Owens

P.O. Box 1254
Sioux Falls, S.D. 57103

March 21, 20__

Public Relations Manager
Bryson Department Store
Fourth & Main Streets
Sioux Falls, S.D. 57114

To the Public Relations Manager:

I would like to submit the enclosed resume for your consideration in hiring the next Customer Service Manager at Bryson. My experience in public relations, marketing, and sales combine to offer you more than the required qualifications listed in your position announcement.

As the Assistant Director for Public Relations at Morris Brothers, I worked closely with consumers who had purchased or were interested in learning more about our products. In cases of complaints from consumers, I quickly and efficiently determined the problem and achieved a solution that met both the consumers' needs and the corporation's goals.

In sales and marketing, I have worked on a variety of market research projects and coordinated targeted promotional campaigns. I have also held supervisory positions in both sales and public relations.

After you have reviewed the enclosed resume, I hope you will call me at 555-3828 so that we can discuss both your expectations and the qualities I can bring to the position. I look forward to an informative discussion.

Sincerely yours,

Judd Riley, Jr.